AF605232

FREDERICK LUIS ALDAMA, SERIES EDITOR

CHESTER BROWN

CHESTER BROWN

FREDERIK BYRN KØHLERT

UNIVERSITY PRESS OF MISSISSIPPI / JACKSON

The University Press of Mississippi is the scholarly publishing agency of the Mississippi Institutions of Higher Learning: Alcorn State University, Delta State University, Jackson State University, Mississippi State University, Mississippi University for Women, Mississippi Valley State University, University of Mississippi, and University of Southern Mississippi.

www.upress.state.ms.us

The University Press of Mississippi is a member of the Association of University Presses.

Any discriminatory or derogatory language or hate speech regarding race, ethnicity, religion, sex, gender, class, national origin, age, or disability that has been retained or appears in elided form is in no way an endorsement of the use of such language outside a scholarly context.

Manufactured in the United States of America
∞

Publisher: University Press of Mississippi, Jackson, USA
Authorised GPSR Safety Representative: Easy Access System Europe - Mustamäe tee 50, 10621 Tallinn, Estonia, gpsr.requests@easproject.com

Library of Congress Cataloging-in-Publication Data

Names: Køhlert, Frederik Byrn, author.
Title: Chester Brown / Frederik Byrn Køhlert.
Description: Jackson : University Press of Mississippi, 2025. | Series: Biographix | Includes bibliographical references and index.
Identifiers: LCCN 2024058201 (print) | LCCN 2024058202 (ebook) | ISBN 9781496858344 (hardback) | ISBN 9781496858351 (trade paperback) | ISBN 9781496858368 (epub) | ISBN 9781496858375 (epub) | ISBN 9781496858382 (pdf) | ISBN 9781496858399 (pdf)
Subjects: LCSH: Brown, Chester, 1960– | Cartoonists—Canada—Biography. | LCGFT: Biographies. | Comics criticism.
Classification: LCC PN6733.B76 Z74 2025 (print) | LCC PN6733.B76 (ebook) | DDC 741.5/971 [B]—dc23/eng/20241209
LC record available at https://lccn.loc.gov/2024058201
LC ebook record available at https://lccn.loc.gov/2024058202

British Library Cataloging-in-Publication Data available

CONTENTS

ACKNOWLEDGMENTS

Thanks to series editor Frederick Luis Aldama for suggesting I write this book; it's been a fun project to work on, and it was a pleasure writing in the format established for the Biographix series. I'm also grateful to Lisa McMurtray at the University Press of Mississippi, who supported the project from the beginning and has been an excellent editor throughout the process. Thanks as well to Nancy Pedri, who first inspired me to undertake some of the research that appears in chapter 6; a much longer version of that chapter was originally written for her edited volume *Comics and Intermediality*, also from the University Press of Mississippi. Parts of the book were written with the support of a residential fellowship from San Cataldo, which enabled me to devote unbroken time to the project, an opportunity I am grateful for.

Several people have provided invaluable help with the research and writing of this book. Dominick Grace has been a supportive interlocutor for my various engagements with Brown's work over the last half decade, and kindly offered his insightful feedback on the manuscript. Brian Campbell and Drawn & Quarterly's Julia Pohl-Miranda provided me with scans of some hard-to-find comics. My brother Lasse Mathiesen Køhlert expertly assisted with getting the book's images into publishable shape. Finally, Chester Brown himself helped me get certain details right and generously shared many images with me, including of the early issues of *Yummy Fur* the minicomic.

Less directly, I am grateful to Ole Birk Laursen for two and a half decades of friendship; our weekly chats and scholarly conversations continue to carry me through difficult personal and professional times. Thanks also to Nicholas Grant for his friendship and unfailing good cheer. I owe the comics reading group I've organized for fifteen years both a special debt of gratitude and much of my ability to think and write about comics: Claudine Gélinas-Faucher, Matthew Jones, Toni Pape, Sara Smith, and Ben Lee Taylor. Similarly, Julian Peters is always ready to talk comics and continues to inspire my work. Kim Davies, finally, is a patient listener yet never afraid of providing a generative challenge when I need it most.

Last but not least, I'm indebted to my family for their love and support: Dorde, Lasse, Nanna, Valdemar, Anders, Christina, and Vitus. A special thanks goes out to Wilfred, whose smile and laughter during our countless games of Cuphead and Spirit Island live on in my heart.

CHESTER BROWN

Figure 0.1. The cover of the 2006 revised edition of *The Little Man.*

Introduction

In the comic drawn for the cover of the 2006 revised edition of *The Little Man*, his collection of short strips originally published between 1980 and 1995, Chester Brown depicts his younger self sitting on the toilet in early 1980, lost in thought (figure 0.1). "What would I do," Brown asks himself, "if that roll of toilet-paper attacked me?"[1] Thinking that this scenario might make for a good story, the nineteen-year-old Chester imagines "a war between toilet-paper and mankind . . . a vast epic—a graphic-novel—maybe two hundred pages long" and proceeds to draw a first panel showing a roll of toilet paper coming to life.[2] As he wonders what should happen next, however, the truth hits him: "what a stupid idea for a story . . . certainly not a good enough idea for a graphic-novel."[3] Although this realization initially gives him pause, Brown continues his musings in the strip's concluding panel: "But maybe it's good enough for a short three or four page strip."

Combined with the new strip drawn for the collection's back cover, in which three small green aliens search for the "planet's greatest cartoonist" and proceed to chat with Brown about the merits of the book, this playfully self-referential paratextual material not only serves to frame the book as consisting at least partly of the author's juvenilia, it also touches upon several major themes that in various ways have been central to Brown's career. These include a fascination with scatology and other taboos, an often idiosyncratic approach to subject matter that has seen him move freely between the epic and the intimate, a predilection for depicting and retroactively commenting on his artistic process, and a habit of abandoning projects that no longer interest him.

Moreover, as the cover strip also suggests to readers familiar with Brown's other work, his more than four-decade-long career has often anticipated or exemplified the shifting trends of alternative comics. In addition to an increasing focus on autobiographical or other reality-based narratives at the expense of genre fiction, these include a shift in publishing format away from serialized comic books found in specialized shops and toward self-contained graphic novels sold in bookstores. From his beginnings selling self-published and often surreal minicomics on consignment through Toronto bookstores, through his serialized alternative comic books *Yummy Fur* (1986–1994) and *Underwater* (1994–1997), to his longer, self-contained narratives *Louis Riel* (2003), *Paying for It* (2011), and *Mary Wept Over the Feet of Jesus* (2016), Brown's career as a whole can be seen as both a microcosm and progenitor of many of the material and thematic developments that have characterized a certain stratum of the comics world since the early 1980s.[4]

With a focus on Brown's place in the changing comics landscape, this book provides a critical account of the life and career of one of the most acclaimed and influential cartoonists of the last half century. For Brown, crucially, his lived experience and artistic work are not always separate spheres, and there is often a great deal of overlap between the two. This is not only because of his substantial autobiographical output but also because Brown has developed a distinctive authorial persona through his many far-ranging interviews, his tendency to habitually redraw and reformat earlier work to better suit his present artistic and intellectual sensibilities, and his unusual and ever-increasing inclusion of notes, appendices, and other supplementary material in his comics. In this material as well as in the comics narratives themselves, both Brown the author and Chester the character often advance contentious opinions. The result is the establishment of a contrarian public persona initially developed in the letter column of *Yummy Fur* and most recently solidified through the many blog posts sent to his supporters on the crowdfunding platform Patreon.[5] When one reads Brown's work, moreover, the artist and his art tend to intersect in unusual ways, and throughout his career he has shown a persistent interest in topics and characters—including, often, himself—that exist outside of the cultural mainstream. To take just two examples: In what are his most well-known works, the historical biography *Louis Riel*, about the nineteenth century Métis leader's armed rebellion against the Canadian government, and *Paying for It*, which is subtitled "a Comic-Strip Memoir about Being a John" and is about Brown's own experiences with sex workers, Brown's main characters (Riel and himself, respectively) are portrayed as being in direct opposition to established political and cultural paradigms. As such, both books explicitly serve to advance an antiauthoritarian worldview rooted in ideas familiar from anarchist and libertarian ideologies. That Brown manages to weave his personal political views into the fabric of two such disparate narratives without losing sight of narrative interest and momentum is a testament to both his skills as a cartoonist and the fundamental relatability of his antiestablishment perspective. In the words of novelist Jonathan Lethem, Brown is "a citizen of the timeless nation of the dissident soul" (131), and it is this nonconformist and often deliberately provocative approach that has infused what is one of the most varied and distinctive bodies of work in all of comics history.

As an independent cartoonist in early 1980s Toronto, Brown's career began at the outskirts of the comics world, geographically as well as thematically. As Dominick Grace and Eric Hoffman write in the introduction to their edited volume titled *The Canadian Alternative*, "Canadian comics have always existed on the edge. Beginning with [eighteenth century caricaturist George] Townshend, Canadian cartoonists react against and exist outside of, if not in opposition to, the dominant milieu" ("Comics in Canada," xii). Noting the "myriad ways that Canadian comics and cartoonists have functioned as alternatives—to American comics, to dominant discourses, even to gender and racial categories" ("Comics in Canada," xv), Grace and Hoffman place Brown in the company of several other unconventional figures from Canadian comics history. These include the pathbreaking 1940s Indigenous female superhero Nelvana of the Northern Lights and feminist artist (and fellow native Quebecer) Julie Doucet, the latter of whose playfully outlandish comics from the 1980s and 1990s have much in common with especially Brown's early work from the same period. In a sweeping attempt to account for the distinctive history of alternative cartooning in Canada, Jeet Heer similarly notes that "cartooning in Canada has always been a matter of survival on the margins," a material circumstance he links to "the special type of individualism that often marks Canadian graphic narrative" ("A Makeshift Tradition," 11). This condition, Heer argues, is emphatically "not the conquering individual on the frontier or the triumphant rags-to-riches hero" familiar from American national narratives, but instead a "contemplative, quirky, self-exploring, solitude-seeking individual" ("A Makeshift Tradition," 12), who is free to experiment in the shadow of a larger and culturally dominant neighbor.

A central figure in both the independent Toronto comics scene and the international alternative tradition of the 1980s and 1990s, Brown has made only very occasional forays into the mainstream comics world. Most notable among these, Brown inked the story "It Came From . . . Higher Space!" written by Alan Moore and penciled by Stephen Bissette for the limited 1993 Image Comics series *1963*. A few such short-lived (but well-paid) experiments with working for hire aside, however, Brown has spent most of his career as a truly independent artist consistently pushing the aesthetic and thematic boundaries of the form, inspired by an unconventional set of impulses grounded in a desire for honesty and truth in representation.[6] As Brown himself has noted about this attitude: "what I wanted to do when I became an artist, was to show life the way I thought it really was. This was my intention. As you actually become an artist you realize how impossible this is. But there's still a feeling that there are certain things in life that you show and certain things you don't show, and I don't want to follow those rules" (qtd. in Solomos, 99). This preoccupation with pushing boundaries and challenging prevailing ideas of what one might expect to find in even an alternative comic book has seen Brown publish several autobiographical narratives that often focus on various aspects of his most intimate moments, complete with frequent and explicit drawings of himself masturbating or having partnered sex. In addition to *Paying for It*, these include *The Playboy* (originally serialized in *Yummy Fur* as "Disgust" and later as "The Playboy Stories"), about his adolescent obsession with *Playboy* magazine, and *I Never Liked You* (originally, and confrontationally, titled "Fuck"), which chronicles both his difficulties with relating to girls during his later teens and his emotionally withdrawn relationship with his mother. At the very beginning of his turn to autobiography, moreover, Brown published two short strips titled "Helder" and "Showing Helder," the second of which details the creation of the first, including critiques by friends that motivate him to change certain aspects. As these examples show, there is seemingly very little about his life that Brown is unwilling to share with his readers, and his work is consistently engaged with the interface between life and art, as well as with the creative process of turning one into the other.

In addition to autobiographical disclosure, the other most prominent subject of Brown's comics is his career-long preoccupation with religious themes. From his early adaptations of the Gospels serialized in the pages of *Yummy Fur* through his retelling of selected Bible stories mostly on the theme of prostitution in *Mary Wept Over the Feet of Jesus*, the endless interpretative potential of Christian scripture has been a rich artistic vein for Brown, and one he has often explored by focusing on the intersection of the sacred with the profane. In his first sustained narrative, which was eventually collected in several varying editions as *Ed the Happy Clown*, Brown mixed classic horror elements like werewolves and vampires with religious imagery and themes—including a masturbating and entirely made up "Saint Justin"—in a surreal stew of narrative antics that also includes literal mountains of shit and a penis whose tip has been replaced with the head of

Ronald Reagan.[7] Although Brown's later engagements with religion have mostly been in a different key, Christianity has continued to play a central role in most of his work, including in depictions of his strict religious upbringing in the earliest autobiographical narratives and in his imaginings of Louis Riel's alleged mystical visions. This preoccupation with religion has so far found its fullest expression in *Mary Wept Over the Feet of Jesus*, a hybrid work consisting roughly of two-parts comics narrative to one-part biblical exegesis as expressed in almost a hundred pages of endnotes and other appendices. While such subject matter can be seen as somewhat incongruous with even the ever-widening world of alternative comics, this work and approach is in perfect alignment with Brown's general impulse to follow his frequently esoteric interests to unexpected destinations.

For Brown, this artistic restlessness has been something of a double-edged sword, and he has made a career-long habit of abandoning work in progress when it no longer captures his full attention. This impulse has been present from the beginning of Brown's career. In addition to the drastically shortened version of "The Toilet Paper Revolt," the very first issue of the self-published minicomic run of *Yummy Fur* consists of a three-page story called "Walrus Blubber Sandwich," which was similarly intended to be a much longer narrative for which Brown had already written a full script. As nonsensical a story as its title indicates, "Walrus Blubber Sandwich" was quickly abandoned once Brown realized that he had no interest in drawing the remaining eighteen pages. Instead, he recalls, "I just had the flying-saucer crash and kill everyone on page three" (*Little Man* [2006], 162). As Brown further notes about his early career, "drawing comics takes discipline, and it took me several years to get to the point where I could tackle longer strips" (*Little Man* [2006], 162). Even after developing the skills and patience needed to create extended narratives, however, Brown has routinely abandoned work in progress. The long list of his unfinished comics includes the initially open-ended saga following Ed the Happy Clown, his planned adaptations of the four Gospels (only "Mark" was finished while "Matthew" remains incomplete), and the main storyline from his series *Underwater*, which follows the slow development of an infant and was something of a creative and commercial failure. For comics artists, who routinely spend several years writing and drawing extended projects, such apparent indifference to the time and effort already invested in a work is more than a little unusual but indicates Brown's unwillingness to go through the motions of finishing work that fails to fully engage him.

Brown's habit of constantly changing his mind about the value and direction of a given project is also related to his unusual method of page composition, by which he draws each panel (or even part thereof) on a separate sheet of paper. First implemented as early as during the composition of "Walrus Blubber Sandwich," this technique not only allows Brown to assemble his narratives as pages after most of the drawing has been completed, it also permits him to easily edit a story by adding, removing, or rearranging panels (or even individual elements thereof) without disrupting the integrity of a finished page.[8] Whether inspired by his tendency to tinker or enabling it in the first place, the method has allowed Brown to consider even his published work as open-ended and subject to continual revision. The result is a body of work that is always in motion and can undergo substantial changes between each new edition, which may be thoroughly reformatted or even partially redrawn. *The Playboy*, for example, was first serialized across three issues of *Yummy Fur* in 1990, then significantly reformatted for a book collection in 1992, before appearing as a revised 2013 edition for which Brown redrew parts of almost every panel while also changing the page layouts, overall book size, and background color from black to white, among several other adjustments. Similarly, the history of the narrative centering on Ed the Happy Clown is particularly convoluted, and in addition to several different book collections it so far includes Brown announcing in 2005 that he was working on an entirely rewritten and redrawn version of a section of the story originally serialized in *Yummy Fur* in the 1980s.

Although this revised edition was ultimately left unfinished and has never seen publication, Brown's dual habits of abandoning and revising work means that almost his entire comics output (at least until his two most recent books, *Paying for It* and *Mary Wept Over the Feet of Jesus*, which have yet to be revised) is either half-finished or exists in multiple different versions. For this reason, most of Brown's comics can be difficult to discuss authoritatively, since the many visual and narrative changes between editions often have important thematic implications.

In this book, I mostly privilege the first-published version of each of Brown's narratives, to allow for a chronological treatment that follows Brown's development from the creator of self-published minicomics to the celebrated author of stand-alone graphic novels. This approach will see me discuss Brown's life and work across five chapters each focusing on a separate part of his career, while also placing each comic in the biographical and cultural contexts in which it first appeared. In order to account for the multiple and often very different editions that exist of most of Brown's comics, the book's sixth chapter provides a critical perspective on his extensive history of revisions, including also a consideration of how Brown has deployed both these and his increasingly voluminous paratextual material in the service of creating a highly distinctive authorial persona that in turn cannot help but influence how we encounter and read his work. With Brown, it can often be nearly impossible to separate the artist from the art, and the intertwining of the two is itself an in-progress concern continually undergoing further revision. This book is an attempt to account for both, including the myriad ways they have informed each other across the last four decades of comics history.

CHAPTER 1

From off the Streets of Toronto Comes

Yummy Fur the Minicomic

When the first self-published issue of *Yummy Fur* the minicomic appeared in various locations across Toronto in July 1983, it entered a comics world in flux. While the "big two," DC and Marvel, had achieved something of a hegemonic stronghold on the mainstream comic book market, a new generation of independently minded artists and publishers were beginning to take advantage of recent advances in printing technologies and distribution methods that together allowed for cheaper production and more experimental content. Variously labelled "alternative," "ground-level," or "the new comics," this new wave grew out of the underground comix movement of the 1960s and 1970s, which had itself thoroughly revolutionized the medium by first establishing it as a credible vehicle for personal expression in both form and content, often controversially so.

By relying on small-scale publishing and distribution through places like head shops and independent book and music stores, the undergrounds also circumvented the industry's often stultifying self-censorship as expressed most notoriously through the 1954 Comics Code Authority, which had been set up in response to the threat of boycotts and political intervention. A similar bypassing of both traditional newsstands and the Code was also a defining feature of a new system of distribution called the direct market, which appeared in the 1970s and enabled publishers to sell their titles directly through monthly preorders to a growing network of specialist comic shops. Under the direct market, the shops gave up the possibility of returning unsold stock in exchange for bulk discounts and other benefits, a system that turned the shops themselves—rather than individual readers—into the final customers of the publishers. Because comics publishers no longer had to estimate the demand for their various titles, the direct market enabled them to not only streamline their print runs, but also to (in theory, at least) take more creative risks on titles aimed at a narrower and more adult readership. Often credited with revitalizing the mainstream publishers, the direct market also encouraged the formation of several smaller publishers, who could take advantage of the new system of distribution to sell directly to shops with much reduced start-up costs and without the threat of censorship. The result was a parallel invigoration of the alternative comics world, which saw an explosion of new publishers and creators in the mid-1980s, attracted to the form by the dual promises of artistic freedom and more predictable finances. Following these developments in publishing and distribution, the comics world in the first half of the 1980s quickly became a hotbed of experimentation that in turn enabled the development of idiosyncratic artistic visions. As Charles Hatfield shows in his authoritative history of the direct market and its effects, "this growth in the alternative press . . . effectively unlocked the comic book's artistic potential" (*Alternative Comics*, 23) by creating an atmosphere where comics could be seen as a viable format for the expression of more adult sensibilities than had typically been the case.

Whether the first issue of *Yummy Fur* the minicomic contains any adult sensibilities is perhaps open to debate, but it is clearly a work inspired by an awareness that making comics can be a grassroots and intentionally eccentric undertaking. The titles of the two short stories making up the eight-page issue—namely "Walrus Blubber Sandwich" and "The Toilet Paper Revolt"—provide an indication of the somewhat juvenile content, and the narratives themselves are underdeveloped and carry the marks of having been shortened or abandoned midway through.[1] Focusing, respectively, on a Toronto restaurateur's attempt to procure walrus blubber for his "arctic cuisine" and the titular revolt, the two stories are crudely but deliberately nonsensical in the tradition of both the undergrounds and many of the new alternative comics of the time. The black and white artwork, on the other hand, is remarkably accomplished and—from a retrospective viewpoint—instantly recognizable as the work of the young Chester Brown. "The Toilet Paper Revolt" is also notable for being one of only a few published examples of Brown using overlapping panels, an approach to page composition he had mostly abandoned in favor of drawing each panel on its own sheet of paper by the time of creating the issue's other story.[2] While skillfully drawn and clearly indebted to the aesthetics and narrative experimentation found in the world of underground and alternative comics, what is entirely missing from these stories is a personal or political viewpoint. As Brown recalls, "most of the underground comic-books focused on three subjects: sex, drugs, and politics," and because he was still a virgin, had tried neither illegal nor legal drugs (with the exception, he deadpans, of "a tiny bit of coffee on one occasion"), and had no interest in politics, he "had good reasons for avoiding those topics" (*Little Man* [2006], 171). Although he was technically proficient and had an evident talent for narrative experimentation, this lack of worldly experience meant that Brown at twenty years old was, in the words of his much older self, "virtually an infant" (*Little Man* [2006], 171), a condition he has linked to both his religious upbringing and to being "a pretty nerdy teenager who got picked on a lot" (qtd. in Juno, 132).[3]

Chester William David Brown was born into an English-speaking family residing in the quiet Montreal suburb of Châteauguay on May 16, 1960. The elder of two brothers, Brown has characterized his upbringing as happy and normal. Brown's father was an electrical engineer while his mother stayed at home, and the family attended church every Sunday. Although Brown had no formal religious training, Christian instruction played a part at his local school, and at home his parents frequently read Bible stories to the children. With a home full of books ranging from James Bond novels to classics of Russian literature, Brown read widely but gravitated toward comics at an early age, and soon began to create his own short strips featuring his family members. Despite growing up in Quebec, Brown had very little exposure to francophone culture, comics or otherwise, and his main early influences were anglophone Canadian newspaper strips like *Doug Wright's Family* and American superhero titles like *Batman*, which his mother would buy for the children whenever she visited the city. As he built a reputation as a talented artist among his family and friends, Brown began to draw his own superhero stories and dreamed of a career as a professional comics artist, inspired also by the Marvel horror comics of the 1970s. Brown's mother passed away in 1976 after a long struggle with schizophrenia, an event and diagnosis that Brown would repeatedly return to in his work. After graduating from high school the following year, Brown made two trips to New York City in 1977 and 1979, where he hoped to break into the comic book industry. Although he had encouraging meetings with editors and art directors at both DC and Marvel, Brown remembers being told that he "didn't draw enough beautiful people" (qtd. in Grammel, 76) for the mainstream comics publishers and returned disappointed to Montreal on both occasions.

In the time between his two trips to New York City, Brown enrolled in Dawson College in Montreal, where he studied commercial art in the hope of improving his drawing skills. Already familiar with alternative comics like *Heavy Metal*, it was during his time at Dawson that Brown first became exposed to the undergrounds, through his friendships with local artists Steve Doucet and Richard Tremblay (better known as Rick Trembles). Doucet and Tremblay were self-publishing zines that included comics by themselves and others from their circle, and soon Brown was contributing stories with titles like "My Friends or The Big Juicy Tit" to *Underground Daze* and *Weird Tales* (figure 1.1). At around the same time as his involvement in the Montreal self-publishing scene, Brown started to read more work by artists such as Robert Crumb and Art Spiegelman and also encountered Will Eisner's *A*

Figure 1.1. An issue of *Weird Tales* with cover art by Brown.

Contract with God. Although he initially found Crumb's comics "disgusting," Brown recalls how this exposure showed him that "there were other kinds of comics that were possible" (qtd. in Grammel, 77), and his interest in breaking into the mainstream comics industry began to wane. After just over a year at Dawson, Brown dropped out because the program did not seem relevant to his aspirations of becoming a professional comics artist. Following his second unsuccessful trip to New York City in 1979, Brown failed to find work in Montreal. When his family shortly after relocated to small-town Ontario, Brown decided to move to Toronto in September of that year, taking a job at a photography lab while spending most of his free time making comics.

Joining the exodus of anglophone Quebecers to other provinces at the time of the political upheavals leading up to and following the 1980 independence referendum, Brown recalls that "since I wanted to become a cartoonist, I thought it might be a good idea to live in the city that is the centre of the English-Canadian publishing world" (*Little Man* [2006], 161). Although Toronto had a lively alternative and small press scene that included pioneering publishers like Coach House Books, it was one of Brown's coworkers at the photography lab who provided his first introduction to that world. After nothing came of an idea to collaborate on a self-published comic, however, Brown started sending his work to the leading American alternative comics publishers and magazines of the time, such as Last Gasp, Rip Off Press, and *Raw*, published by Spiegelman and Françoise Mouly. Upon submitting a story called "City Swine" to *Raw*, Brown recalls how a handwritten note on the form rejection letter let him know that they had almost published it, but had concluded that "we think you can do better, so send more stuff" (qtd. in Moreton et al., 4). With unpublished work piling up, it was not until Brown's girlfriend Kris encouraged him to simply self-publish his comics that the idea materialized.

Needing a title that could encompass a broad range of stories without a central theme or character, Brown decided on *Yummy Fur* and in July 1983 printed a run of 150 copies of the first eight-page issue, which he attempted to sell by himself on the streets of Toronto for twenty-five cents, using the imprint Tortured Canoe (figure 1.2). When he failed to sell even a single copy on his first day, however, Brown changed his approach and instead found

Figure 1.2. The cover of the first issue of *Yummy Fur* the minicomic.

success selling his comic on consignment through local comic shops, bookstores, and music stores, which in turn plugged him into the world of mail-order zines and minicomics. Encouraged by the positive response and his newfound community, Brown immediately printed a second issue of *Yummy Fur* later that same month, followed by a third issue in August and a fourth issue expanded to twelve pages in September. Functioning as something of a clearinghouse for the many short comics he had produced in the years since moving to Toronto, the first four issues of the minicomic appeared in rapid succession, and the momentum helped Brown quickly build a growing readership that in turn led to several more printings of each issue over the next year.

By the time issues 5 and 6 came out in January and April 1984, *Yummy Fur* was enough of a success that Brown was invited by local curator Michael Merrill (himself a sometimes-independent cartoonist) from the ChromaZone collective to contribute to the Kromalaffing exhibition at Toronto's Grunwald Gallery in February of that year. Featuring work by many of the leading alternative comics artists associated with *Raw*, including Gary Panter, Charles Burns, and Joost Swarte, as well as Spiegelman himself, the exhibition also included work by such figures as Harvey Pekar and several local Toronto-area cartoonists. The exhibition catalogue reprinted a few pages by each artist, and the added exposure led to Brown being invited to submit work to such anthology comics as *Escape*, *Casual Casual*, and *Dada Gumbo*. For *Dada Gumbo*, Brown contributed a one-page short story called "Things to Avoid Stepping On," which in its first panel featured a very detailed close-up drawing of a dog shit. When the issue's editor replied that Brown had put him "in the awkward position of having to admit that I find it offensive" (qtd. in Brown *Little Man* [2006], 165) and asked him to consider replacing the image with something else, this reaction so amused Brown that it inspired him to compose an entire two-page story devoted to scatology. Appearing in the seventh and final issue of the minicomic run of *Yummy Fur*, which due to Brown's success in placing work elsewhere was published

Figure 1.3. "The Man Who Couldn't Stop," from issue 7 of *Yummy Fur* the minicomic (reprinted in all three book collections of *Ed the Happy Clown*).

with some delay in September 1985, "The Man Who Couldn't Stop" features ten near-identical panels of a single character sitting on a toilet (figure 1.3).[4] In the final panel, the strip ends when the Man looks down between his legs with a concerned look on his face, noting that he cannot seem to stop. In addition to being an early example of Brown's recalcitrant reaction to even a polite request for content moderation, "The Man Who Couldn't Stop" is notable as one of the points where an unlikely larger narrative gradually begins to coalesce from the many different stories published in *Yummy Fur* the minicomic.

For the first few years of Brown's career, his many different stories were conceived as stand-alone pieces with no obvious or intended narrative thread connecting them. Short, offbeat, and often outright nonsensical, the stories appearing in both the minicomic and the various anthologies Brown contributed to often give the impression of being the product of an eccentric artistic imagination almost wholly unconcerned with traditional narrative features or any semblance to real-world characters or subjects. In the one-page story "Mars," for example, which appeared in the second issue of *Yummy Fur*, the first panel shows a man and a woman in front of a spacecraft taking off (figure 1.4). After the woman exclaims "Doctor—your plan worked!! The earthmen have left Mars never to return!!," the man replies with "Yes . . . I wonder how I did it?" before continuing in the next panel: "Well—no matter—now I can devote my time to my *true* interests!" Incongruously, one of these turns out to be sea serpents, and the rest of the page consists of a series of unconnected panels depicting the characters looking for—but not finding—sea serpents in various locations, before it abruptly ends with the man muttering "Let's go home" (*Yummy Fur* #3, 8; emphasis in the original).[5] As Brown recalls, "Mars" was composed by standing in front of his comic book collection with his eyes closed, picking up comics and pointing at panels at random until he had enough for a full page. Redrawing these in his own hand and trying "to write some kind of story (to use the word loosely) around the images," Brown "was pleased with the result and frequently used this technique to kick-start myself creatively on other strips" (*Little Man* [2006], 162). Other stories composed at least partially in this way include "About Brad's Enlightenment" published in *Casual Casual* and "I Live in the Bottomless Pit" from the seventh issue of *Yummy Fur*, but Brown soon supplanted this experimental method of generating narrative with a more fully conceptualized approach based on surrealist principles of spontaneous creation.

During the summer of 1982, Brown remembers, "I was concerned that I hadn't been producing enough finished pages, so I decided to create more spontaneously" (*Ed* [2012], 205). In this, Brown was inspired by Wallace Fowlie's *Age of Surrealism*, which he describes as showing how surrealist writers inspired by Freud "believed that in creating spontaneously they could get in touch with The Unconscious and were thus producing work that were in

Figure 1.4. "Mars," from the second issue of *Yummy Fur* the minicomic (reprinted in *The Little Man*).

some way meaningful, even if it read like meandering nonsense" (*Ed* [2012], 205). As Brown drolly continues, he "was many years away from coming to the conclusion that Freud was wrong about most things, so this surrealist stuff sounded valid" (*Ed* [2012], 205–6). Although Fowlie "made spontaneous creation sound like an interesting idea" (*Ed* [2012], 206), Brown was not inspired to seek out any of the writing produced by the surrealists, electing instead to transfer the principles to comics-making according to his own method.

Doing away with writing scripts in favor of panel-by-panel improvisation, Brown's first experiment with spontaneous creation was a short six-page story titled "Ed the Happy Clown," which was eventually published the following summer in the second issue of *Yummy Fur*. "Supposed to be complete in itself" and "just a bit of silliness that I hoped would be amusing to somebody" (*Ed* [2012], 206), the narrative follows two main strands, one of which centers on the eponymous Ed. Introduced while on his way to visit sick children in the hospital, Ed is informed in the next panel that "the hospital burned down and everyone died except us doctors" (*Yummy Fur* #3, 3). Changing his plans, Ed suddenly (and without cause) breaks his leg in three places at once on his way to an orphanage. Immediately hereafter, Ed is attacked by hungry-looking rats, who have already been introduced in the second narrative strand when a diminutive professor delivers a report on the city's rat problem to the mayor. Putting their rat-control plan into action, the mayor and the professor drop a group of "rat eating pygmies from a rodent infested third world country" from an airplane, which leads to a disturbing moment when the reader is informed that "there's no picture for this panel however there are some sound effects: Splut . . . Splat . . . Splrtch" (*Yummy Fur* #3, 6, 7).[6] As the pygmies die upon impact, the narrative shifts back to Ed, who with great relief exclaims that "the rats are attacking those dead babies" (*Yummy Fur* #3, 7). The story ends with a final panel depicting the airplane circling while the mayor notes that something seems to have gone wrong, to which the professor replies with a "shucks darn!!" (*Yummy Fur* #3, 7). Across thirteen panels of bad taste and several sudden narrative and tonal shifts, the story carries the unmistakable imprint of having been improvised, but it is testament to Brown's quickly developing skills as a cartoonist that the result is not only intelligible but arguably rises at least somewhat above the "meandering nonsense" mentioned in Brown's assessment of surrealist writing.

Because the story was a result of his experimentation with spontaneous creation, Brown never intended to return to its characters. As he recalls, "for all I knew I'd never draw Ed the happy clown again" (*Ed* [2012], 206), but the experience was still so successful in helping him generate material that Brown relied on this method for several other strips. In a characteristically candid assessment, Brown has said about this moment in his career that "embracing surrealistic spontaneous creation gave me an artistic direction at a time when, to be frank, I had nothing to say" (*Ed* [2012], 206). Despite his new interest in prioritizing surreal stream-of-consciousness over thematic coherency and straightforward narrative momentum, Brown nevertheless soon found himself returning not only to Ed but also to several other characters and scenarios first introduced in this and other early stories. Prominent among these is a series of strips each called "Adventures in Science," in which various scientists study phenomena such as "the giant squids [sic] masturbation techniques" (*Yummy Fur* #4, 10), the appearance of "the likeness of the face of Jesus Christ on an ordinary piece of masking tape" (*Yummy Fur* #6, 2), and the best method for distinguishing between "a common earthworm and a concert grand piano" (*Yummy Fur* #7, 5). Although most of these scientific inquiries take unexpected turns and remain largely unexplored, the frequent appearance of scientists would become something of a recurring theme. As these and other stories proliferated, the initially separate universes contained in *Yummy Fur* began to cross-pollinate each other as characters originally introduced in one strip would make a habit of suddenly appearing halfway through another.

In the story "Ed and the Beanstalk," for example, first published in issue 4, the narrative initially focuses on a couple named Jack and Tilley, who have to sell their cow because they are out of food. Brown had begun the strip as "Jack and the . . ." in 1981 but abandoned it after finishing the first page. A few years later, Brown decided to return to the story and replaced the page's final panel with a caption saying "elsewhere" and a drawing of Ed lost somewhere in "the void" (*Yummy Fur* #5, 2). Reintroducing the character was motivated by positive response from the readers to the previous Ed story, and as the void turns outs to exist only as a bad dream for Ed, the strip continues to follow him for a few pages. Switching between different improvisational techniques, Brown first introduces Ed's friend Christian and brings back the now reanimated and sewer-dwelling pygmies, before abruptly moving to a drawing of "Frankenstein" (the monster), a change in direction that was prompted by Brown pulling out a random comic book from his collection that happened to feature that character.[7] As Frankenstein visits Jack and Tilley and Christian starts eating the pygmies, all narrative coherence at first seems lost, but in its place something like a recurring set of characters and a recognizable (but unpredictable) world has started to appear from the improvised parts.

By the time "The Man Who Couldn't Stop" appeared in the seventh and final issue of the minicomic run of *Yummy Fur*, by now expanded to twenty-four pages, Brown had started to find a narrative groove that retroactively connected many of his existing stories and characters. Despite the fact that its initial inspiration was a request for less scatology in a different strip, "The Man Who Couldn't Stop" was never intended as a stand-alone piece and Brown always knew that the character would return elsewhere. This return occurs just a few pages later in the same issue, where the character is brought into the longest installment yet of the extended Ed narrative. Unable to stop defecating but realizing that he is going to run out of space, the Man leaves the public washroom and is soon spotted by one of the "Adventures in Science" scientists, who mistakes him for a werewolf because of the odor and the growing bulge at the back of his pants. After the scientist attacks the Man in a preemptive attempt at self-defense, both are taken to jail where they are placed in a cell next to Ed. Having himself been arrested after being falsely accused of cutting off and stealing the hand of a hospital janitor named Chet in a previous strip, Ed is subsequently freed when the ever-accumulating feces from the cell next door breaks the walls and destroys the jail.[8]

With this unsettling and disgustingly over-the-top series of events, the minicomic run of *Yummy Fur* ended. Brown would soon continue the story in a more professional publication format, but as seen together, the seven self-published issues are a fascinating example of how the 1980s alternative scene provided a set of material conditions that enabled not only the gradual development of an extended narrative based on surrealist and scatological absurdity, but also an invaluable self-directed apprenticeship in comics-making for one of the era's most idiosyncratic artistic sensibilities.

CHAPTER 2

Sacred Profanities

Ed the Happy Clown and the Gospel Adaptations

In a March 1985 cover story for the *Comics Journal*, critic and associate editor Dale Luciano took stock of the recent upsurge in self-published minicomics. After some initial hesitation, Luciano accepts the awkward but at the time much bandied-about term "newave" to describe these comics, while taking pains both to distinguish it from "new wave" music and to make it clear that it "is *not* a movement organized around a particular 'school' or [sic] art or a shared set of political attitudes or assumptions" (52; emphasis in the original). Instead, Luciano argues, "newave" is "best regarded as a catch-all term referring to the hundreds of mostly self-published comix being sold, traded, or otherwise exchanged through the mails by a surprisingly diverse group of comix artists" (52). Although he concludes that "if there is a single distinguishing hallmark of 'newave' comix, it is their close association with the act of self-publication" (52), Luciano's repeated use of the word "comix" also suggests that he perceives a direct influence by the underground comix of the 1960s and 1970s on this new crop of cartoonists. As Luciano himself notes about this influence, "most newave artists work with satirical intent, and [a] substantial number of observers regard the 'newave' as carrying on the tradition of the underground press" (53). Citing the classic example of Robert Crumb self-publishing and selling the first issue of *Zap Comix* on the streets of Berkeley, Luciano establishes a genealogy that he later deploys as an interpretative tool in this treatment of most of the dozens of featured artists. One of these is Chester Brown, who at the time had self-published six issues of *Yummy Fur*. In Luciano's assessment, "Brown's comix are a funny admixture of genre parody and social satire" that distill "the absurdist essence of a 'plot' and presents the incidents as lunatic events within a logical structure," and the writeup as a whole is a remarkably thoughtful and largely positive assessment of "the unpredictable dada world" (60) of *Yummy Fur* the minicomic.[1]

Being featured in the *Comics Journal* represented an important moment in Brown's career. By far the most important publication devoted to news and criticism of nonmainstream comics, the *Journal* printed its first issue in 1977 and was a leading voice in promoting the post-underground world of alternative-minded comics throughout the 1980s and 1990s. Branching out to comics publishing under the name Fantagraphics in 1979, the company was also responsible for issuing some of the era's most influential work, including *Love and Rockets* by the Hernandez brothers and *Eightball* by Daniel Clowes. Although the combination of comics publisher and leading critical organ had its detractors, the arrangement worked out well for Brown, who was invited to contribute work to the Fantagraphics anthology comic *Honk!* after its editor read about *Yummy Fur* in the Luciano article. Brown submitted a typically absurd story titled "The Gourmets from Planet X" that featured snot-eating aliens, missing noses, and the devil, and with Fantagraphics paying thirty dollars per page the occasion represented the first time he was paid directly to create comics as an adult.[2] This was both a welcome and long-overdue development for Brown, who had been growing increasingly weary of self-publishing around the time he put the seventh issue of the *Yummy Fur* minicomic together in the summer of 1985. Although the series had been relatively successful on its own terms, with some issues selling over a thousand copies, Brown recalls being "afraid that writing and drawing comics was only going to be a hobby" (*Ed* [2012], 214) and that he would never be able to quit his day job at the photography lab.

While the Luciano writeup helped open the door to paid work for Brown, it was not until the *Comics Journal* published a very positive review of *Yummy Fur*'s seventh issue in April 1986 that his career began to take off. Calling Brown "one of the smartest minds in comix today" and the issue itself both "one of the most accomplished titles in the burgeoning small-press movement" and "as good as many of the top undergrounds of yesteryear" (54, 55), the review by Steve Monaco caught the eye of Toronto publisher Bill Marks, whose company Vortex Comics was experiencing some success with black-and-white alternative comic books in the new space enabled by the direct market system of distribution. Already familiar with the *Yummy Fur* minis from the local Toronto scene, Marks offered Brown his own series of a professionally published bimonthly comic book, also to be called *Yummy Fur*. Brown accepted the offer, and the first three issues consisted of reprints from the minicomics.[3]

After preorders for the first issue of the Vortex run of *Yummy Fur* numbered over twelve thousand in the fall of 1986, Brown immediately quit his day job and set to work creating new material for the fourth issue, scheduled for April 1987.[4] Having spent several years on the stories collected in the first three issues, Brown realized the necessity of learning to generate material faster now that he was the creator of a comic book set to appear regularly every other month. As he recalls, "I knew I'd have to produce quickly to put out six issues a year, so I decided that continuing stories made sense, rather than beginning something new each issue" (qtd. in Evenson, 115). With a larger narrative centering on Ed the Happy Clown having gradually started to appear by the end of the minicomic run, Brown made the decision to continue that storyline in the Vortex series.

Not yet named after its main character, the lead story in the fourth (but first all-new) issue of *Yummy Fur* is a nineteen-page installment of the Ed saga titled simply "Forgiven." Introducing several new characters while tying together numerous loose ends from the minis, this section of the extended narrative was a major creative step forward for Brown. After the story begins with a single image of Chet the janitor being questioned by the police about his previously missing (but later limply reattached) hand, the very next panel announces that we are now in "the thirteenth century" (*Yummy Fur* #4, 2).[5] The following few pages tell the relatively uncomplicated story of a man named Justin whose hand is cut off by his wife after she catches him masturbating.[6] Presented without further commentary but ending with a final image showing a severed hand, the connection to the storyline concerning Chet's missing hand is narratively tenuous but thematically suggestive. Switching, suddenly, to an unspecified point in "the twentieth century" (*Yummy Fur* #4, 5), the story continues with a short sequence showing Chet as a child, having the story of "Saint Justin" read to him by his mother.[7] According to the mother's copy of "Lives of the Saints," Justin was a thief who after a religious vision "cut off his own right hand" in order to follow Jesus's teaching that "if thy hand offend thee cut it off—it is better to enter into life maimed than having two hands to go into hell" (*Yummy Fur* #4, 6). Although an accurate representation of a passage from Mark 9:43, this line creates an immediate dissonance by putting into question the issue of how exactly Justin lost his hand. The implication of the discrepancy between the visually presented story of Justin and the secondhand narrative recounted in "Lives of the Saints" appears to be that Christian myths are at best unreliable and at worst entirely made up in the service of religious moral instruction. In the context of an alternative comic book that had until now largely been concerned with scatology and narrative absurdity, the first few pages of *Yummy Fur*'s fourth Vortex issue thereby suddenly introduced an unexpected religious dimension into the ongoing narrative, and one that seemed like it might have thought-provoking things to say about the nature of Christianity itself.

Flashing forward to "about thirty years later" (*Yummy Fur* #4, 7), the following section continues in this vein. As an adult Chet wearing a monk's robe prays in front of a statue of the Virgin

Mary holding a baby Jesus, the statue comes alive in the figure of a young woman who seduces Chet, before—in the middle of intercourse—she violently pulls off his hand while moaning "ooh . . . Saint . . . Justin!" (*Yummy Fur* #4, 9). This sequence, in turn, is immediately revealed to be a dream of Chet's, and as he wakes up it becomes clear that the figure from the dream is a woman named Josie, with whom Chet is having an extramarital affair. After visiting the hospital to have his reattached hand examined, Chet next comes across the story of Saint Justin in a bookstore before making plans to meet Josie again later that night. While the two have sex in a park, Chet explains that it was God who made his hand fall off because "he had to be shocked into recognizing the sinful state . . . of my life" (*Yummy Fur* #4, 19). Remembering "the lesson of Saint Justin . . . that you have to cut from yourself the thing that is making you sin" (*Yummy Fur* #4, 19), Chet suddenly pulls out a knife and stabs Josie to death, an action that has the immediate effect of healing his hand (figure 2.1). A shockingly violent and disturbing conclusion to the issue's installment of the ongoing narrative, the sequence seems to simultaneously suggest the danger of blindly following Christian doctrine while also taking a religious worldview seriously enough to present an instance of miraculous bodily healing as a matter-of-fact occurrence. This thematic instability is mirrored narratively, as the nineteen-page section moves between biblical tales, dream sequences, and flashbacks with a bewildering volatility. Visually, too, Brown's sparse drawings dominated by heavy blacks create an unsettling atmosphere and the overall impression that the story takes place in an unpredictable moral universe guided by unclear religious principles.

After this installment of the main storyline ends with a violent cliffhanger depicting a murder committed in the name of a Christian God, the issue's very next page is something of a left turn (figure 2.2). On a beautifully composed page-wide panel showing a starry sky and a lone serene-looking figure, a title announces "Mark: Part One" and a caption reads "the begining [sic] of the good news of Jesus Christ" (*Yummy Fur* #4, 21). Accompanied by a

Figure 2.1. Chet kills Josie, from *Ed the Happy Clown* (originally published in *Yummy Fur* #4).

Figure 2.2. The first page of "Mark," from *Yummy Fur* #4 (uncollected).

small note explaining that the story is "an adaptation of the biblical book" (*Yummy Fur* #4, 21), the issue's remaining pages are made up of the first section of Brown's retelling of the Gospel of Mark. At this point, any *Yummy Fur* reader who has made it through the rest of the issue would be forgiven for expecting a Brown adaptation of the Bible to be infused with the same offbeat energy and unpredictable narrative maneuvers as the main storyline. Indeed, the juxtaposition of violent religious murder with "the good news of Jesus Christ" is so unexpected that it initially seems like something of a narrative stunt that will eventually see Brown fold this sequence into his principal narrative in order to develop and further complicate its already ambiguous engagement with Christianity. Instead, the short section of "Mark" presented at the end of the issue is a remarkably conventional and visually restrained retelling of the familiar story, in which Brown relies largely on narrative captions (a feature almost entirely missing from the rest of the issue) to give his faithful but abridged adaptation the overall feel of a traditional illustrated Bible story. Brown himself has said about his approach that he "was trying to distance the reader" (qtd. in Grammel, 87), and whereas the Ed storyline is drawn in a dynamic style that fluidly switches between closeups and more zoomed-out depictions of events from a variety of angles, the visual universe of "Mark" favors a combination of medium and long shots, often viewed slightly from above, which creates the effect of a certain reverence for the source material. Brian Evenson argues about Brown's decision to retell the story in this way that "it comes across as weirder than something truly weird would be" since "it makes us shift our expectations as readers, taking away what we thought we knew about Brown as a storyteller" (57). At the time of *Yummy Fur*'s fourth issue, certainly, very few readers would have expected the author of "The Man Who Couldn't Stop" to engage with Christian scripture in any but the most satirical or glib capacity.

While Brown had a very religious upbringing and grew up considering himself a Christian, his beliefs were largely unexamined until he was in his early twenties. Even after he stopped attending church on a regular basis when moving to Toronto, Brown remained religious in what he has later called "a vague way," despite the fact that he "really didn't have a clear idea of what Christianity was about" (*Ed* [2012], 217). As Brown became increasingly interested in learning about what he calls his "Christian roots," however, he started reading widely about Christianity and also returned to the Bible itself, immersing himself "in these words that had such a deep impact on my life, the formation of who I am" (qtd. in McConnell, 208). Because much of his reading "came from a literary textual-analysis point-of-view that made the Judeo-Christian Scriptures seem like just a mish-mash of different people's contradictory theological ideas with no consistent, coherent philosophy" (*Ed* [2012], 217), Brown's faith was weakened, but he instead developed a strong interest in both the textual history of the Bible and the historical figure of Jesus. Recalling that "atheism was too strong a pill for me to swallow" (*Ed* [2012], 217), Brown settled on calling himself an agnostic, and embarking on an adaptation of the Gospels was therefore an extension of this personal project and a way to engage with Christianity as an adult and on its own terms, in order to figure out what he believed.

The initial installment of "Mark" that rounds out the fourth issue of *Yummy Fur* is only six pages long, but Brown featured the Gospel adaptations throughout the entire thirty-two-issue run and also continued them in the shorter-lived successor *Underwater*. Appearing, with a few exceptions, in short sections of varying length at the back of each issue, both "Mark" and the subsequent (but unfinished) adaptation of "Matthew" were an integral part of Brown's comics output for more than a decade, making them his longest-running extended narrative.[8] In the early issues, especially, Brown appeared to relish the potential for unexpected and incongruous thematic interplay between the Ed the Happy Clown installments and the Gospel adaptations, occasionally even switching from one narrative to the other halfway down the page and from one panel to the next. In addition to giving Brown what he has called "a lot of latitude from the perspective of filling an issue" (qtd. in Evenson, 111), the continuing Gospel adaptations thereby often appear to be in implicit dialogue with the more freewheeling primary narrative, although the relationship between the two is never made explicit or otherwise remarked upon. In addition to amplifying the religious dimensions of the Ed material, however, one effect of this cross-pollination is that the outwardly more "realistic" and serious-minded Gospel adaptations gradually start to seem like they inhabit a storyworld inspired by an equally baroque imagination, in which such fantastic elements as miracles, demons, and the ability to walk on water are both unquestioned and neutrally represented.

Although Brown never let his Gospel adaptations slip into parody, his deepening personal interest in Christianity and increasing confidence as a cartoonist meant that they became gradually more idiosyncratic in both form and content. As Brown made clear in an interview conducted at the time, this development was at least partly by design, and because his original plan was to adapt all four Gospels and in this way "tell it over another three times . . . starting from a traditional view seemed like a good place to start. And I can get weirder as I go along" (qtd. in Grammel, 86). Consequently, while "Mark" is a relatively compact and unfussy narrative serialized across just over two years, by the time the first installment of "Matthew" appeared in issue 15 of *Yummy Fur*, published in March 1989, Brown's approach was markedly different. Using a fuller range of framings and storytelling devices, such as close-ups and lengthy wordless sequences suggesting the mystical dimensions of the material, "Matthew" is a much more dynamically told narrative, with the characters brought more vividly to life. Whereas Jesus himself had in "Mark" been drawn to look and behave like traditional representations and appeared almost exclusively from a deferential distance, in "Matthew" Brown depicted his increasingly iconoclastic main character as a sharp-featured and balding man, who is often scowling angrily at his doubtful and sometimes even faithless disciples. The dialogue, similarly, is highly contemporized and frequently departs from the expected, such as when an angry John the Baptist addresses a group of Pharisees and Sadducees with "You fucking vipers! Do you really expect me to baptize *you* in the Jordan?" (*Yummy Fur* #17, 16) (figure 2.3). Overall, the world of "Matthew" is markedly grubbier and its people are less well-behaved and more grotesquely drawn. As the loutish and acne-prone disciples pick their noses and grope female servers, however, it is clear that Brown's approach in "Matthew" is animated not only by a desire to simply "get weird," but also by an aspiration to humanize the characters by going against the grain of idealizing and bloodless convention.

Over the course of the completed twenty-four installments of "Matthew," Brown gradually began to use the untraditional and sometimes outright eccentric page layouts that became a hallmark of his style in the early nineties (see chapter 3). Elizabeth Rae Coody argues about the visual restraint and traditional narrative approach of "Mark" that "Brown's rigidly square frames consistently suggest an infinite number of possible tellings" (109), and in comparison the much looser narrative and visual styles of "Matthew" give the impression of being rooted firmly in the realm of singular personal interpretation. These narrative and stylistic developments are echoed in Brown's approach to the story itself, which gradually begins to depart from both canonical scripture and traditional interpretations thereof. Starting in "Mark," such departures include a few instances where Brown incorporates short passages from a gnostic text and even inserts events recounted in Morton Smith's controversial *The Secret Gospel*.[9] From the very first installment of "Matthew," moreover, Brown is playing fully against tradition whenever possible, electing for example to depict only two wise men (or "magi") because the text never specifies a number.[10]

Inspired also by his reading of such books as Smith's *Jesus the Magician* and Jane Schaberg's *The Illegitimacy of Jesus*, Brown's Gospel adaptations display an increasing skepticism toward established dogma that reflects his changing relationship to both his

Figure 2.3. John the Baptist addresses the Pharisees and Sadducees in "Matthew," from *Yummy Fur* #17 (uncollected).

own faith and Christianity more broadly conceived. As such, the narratives served their intended purpose of helping Brown decide what he believed, functioning as what Ng Suat Tong in a review in the *Comics Journal* calls "exploratory devices with a very selfish purpose" (37). So successful were the adaptations in this regard that Brown, in a 1990 interview, could say that "by this time I've pretty much worked it out of me. I mean, I can say Jesus wasn't divine without worrying whether I'll go to hell or not. That probably wasn't the case five years ago" (qtd. in Grammel, 88). That the two narratives are also rich and rewarding engagements with the Gospels is evidence both of Brown's technical skills as a cartoonist and his talent for breathing new life into such well-known material through his increasingly irreverent and offbeat approach. Despite having spent over a decade working consistently on the two adaptations, however, Brown has in a more recent interview called them "poorly done" (qtd. in Evenson, 124) and has frequently expressed his lack of interest in finishing "Matthew" or publishing the existing narratives in collected editions.[11] For this reason, Brown also never began work on his planned adaptations of the Gospels of Luke and John, and after he abandoned both "Matthew" and the lead *Underwater* narrative following that title's eleventh issue (see chapter 4), the adaptations remain unfinished and uncollected, available only in the long out-of-print issues of *Yummy Fur*.

In comparison, while the narrative focusing on Ed the Happy Clown only continued until the eighteenth issue of *Yummy Fur*, published in October 1989, its central storyline has been collected in several editions and remains a Harvey Award–winning classic of 1980s alternative comics.[12] As Brown found a more direct outlet for his personal engagement with Christianity in the Gospel adaptations, however, the Ed narrative only intermittently returned to the explicitly religious themes introduced by the story of Saint Justin and Chet's murder of Josie. In their place, Brown followed his imagination in new directions, improvising a story that became increasingly elaborate with each new issue and featured characters such as vampires, aliens, and a miniature Ronald Reagan from another dimension. As part of the story's most notorious plot point, this character is introduced after it is discovered that The Man Who Couldn't Stop's anal opening functions as a portal to another dimension. Although similar to the main dimension in most ways, this is a miniature dimension where toilets have not been invented, and The Man Who Couldn't Stop's condition is the direct effect of its people stuffing their human excrement into the portal as a matter of waste disposal. When the miniature version of Reagan inspects the fecal chute pointing at the portal, he trips and falls into it, causing his head to enter the main dimension and attach itself to Ed's penis under unclear circumstances (figure 2.4). Although no more nonsensical or crass than much of the rest of the story, these particular events became something of a calling card for the series, and served to indicate the lengths Brown was apparently willing to go to—not to mention the things he was willing to draw—in his commitment to distasteful and often outright provocative absurdity. As the story continues, Ed and a highly displeased Reagan intersect with several other old and new characters in unexpected ways, including a reanimated but newly vampiric Josie, the sewer-dwelling pygmies, and the "Adventures in Science" scientists. Repeatedly backing up on itself and providing new perspectives on events originally published several issues earlier, most of the extended narrative is a tour de force for Brown, who masterfully keeps tying everything together while continuing to introduce new developments.

Although the story itself continued at full steam and always included a surprise or two in every issue, after several years of constant narrative reversals and repeated attempts to outgross itself, the ongoing saga gradually but perhaps inevitably began to feel less fresh. More than half a decade in, what was at the outset an exciting and taboo-breaking experiment in narrative form had to Brown himself begun to seem forced and directionless. While its serialized nature and overall open-endedness had initially provided him with an opportunity to follow his impulses in any direction and—in principle, at least—extend the story indefinitely, Brown

Figure 2.4. Ronald Regan appears, from *Ed the Happy Clown* (originally published in *Yummy Fur* #6).

eventually concluded that the material had run its course and quickly wrapped it up in issue 18. As Brown has noted about the decision, although his "original intention had been to just continue on with Ed the Happy Clown as a character forever, like Batman or Superman," he eventually "reached a point where I realized that I didn't want to do that for the rest of my career, and that's when I decided to end it" (qtd. in Epp, 131). This decision coincided approximately with the first book edition of *Ed the Happy Clown*, which was published by Vortex in August 1989 and collected most of the Ed material from the minis through to issue 12 of the comic book. Although the narrative continued for a further six issues of *Yummy Fur*, Brown eventually came to believe that the story should have ended with issue 12, and the subsequent book editions from 1992 and 2012, as well as a 2005 reserialization, contain an only slightly expanded version of the original 1989 collection that jettisons nearly all of the later installments.

Unambiguously stating in a late-career interview that the Ed material from issues 13 to 18 of *Yummy Fur* "sucks" (qtd. in Evenson, 125), Brown is wholly at ease with the fact that yet another large chunk of his work—representing a full year's work on his comic's lead storyline—is now long out of print.[13] Indeed, contrary to the Gospel adaptations, which became more stylistically adventurous and thematically complex with each issue, the later Ed installments seem in retrospect like a classic case of diminishing returns. Where the early sections abound in the charm of watching a skilled cartoonist develop and tie the many different strands of his improvised narrative together, the abandoned material appears decidedly less inspired in its more deliberate structure and calculated provocations. Seeing the two variously unfinished and abandoned narratives together, however, one gets the impression that the initially much looser and anything-goes approach of Ed gradually began to seep into the traditional Bible stories, transforming both them and Brown's relationship to his faith into something more vibrant and fully alive to itself. Brown has said about the collected *Ed the Happy Clown* that although it "wasn't a conscious decision from the beginning . . . the work probably ended up with the theme of how unfair I thought a world run by a Christian god would be" (qtd. in Juno, 135). In that light, the two extended narratives appear to be in an almost interdependent symbiotic relationship in the pages of *Yummy Fur*, with the comic book itself functioning as a kind of laboratory for Brown's narrative experiments. Viewed at a distance, these experiments can themselves be seen as both an important step in Brown's developing interest in using his art for self-examination and as a foreshadowing of his eventual turn to autobiography.[14]

While the first Vortex issue of *Yummy Fur* had seen remarkably high preorders for a black-and-white alternative comic book during the fall of 1986, the series experienced uneven sales for much of its early run.[15] Even as Brown was quickly making a name for himself with the minicomics, the initial preorder numbers of the forthcoming title were less a reflection of intense reader anticipation than a result of fortuitous timing. When it was first self-published in May 1984, the surprise runaway success of Kevin Eastman and Peter Laird's satirical *Teenage Mutant Ninja Turtles* sparked an intense interest in black-and-white comic books that led to publishers and comic shops taking chances on countless new titles in the hope of finding the next big thing. This situation initially led to overproduction and what has become known in the comics world as "the black-and-white glut," but the first issue of *Yummy Fur* had the good fortune of arriving at a time when it briefly seemed possible—to artists, publishers, and shop owners alike—to make a decent living making and selling alternative comic books. The boom lasted for a little over two years, and when the bubble burst and the market started to self-correct in early 1987, preorders for *Yummy Fur* declined sharply and plateaued around two thousand copies for the next few issues.

An additional blow came when, in August 1987, the market-dominant Diamond Comic Distributors suddenly stopped carrying *Yummy Fur*. While the official reason for the decision was the title's relatively low order numbers, Brown has pointed out that the distributor continued to carry other Vortex comics with even lower numbers and has speculated that the real motive was that "someone at Diamond found the content of my comic-book offensive" (*Ed* [2012], 239). As a result, sales of *Yummy Fur* declined even further, reaching a nadir of just under seventeen hundred preorders for issue 9. At a royalty rate of 13.5 percent on a comic book priced at US $1.75 ($2.25 in Canada), Brown made only US $395.25 on the issue. With such precipitous sales, Brown briefly considered ending the title but instead secured a part-time day job to help him make ends meet. When Diamond finally resumed distribution in the summer of 1988, sales of *Yummy Fur* gradually rebounded and eventually climbed to nearly seven thousand per issue at the time when the narrative featuring Ed the Happy Clown wrapped up, a number providing Brown with a steady and livable income.[16]

As a rare survivor of the 1980s boom and bust of alternative comics, *Yummy Fur* continued publication for an additional five years and fourteen issues after Brown concluded the Ed material. Although the serialization of the Gospel adaptations continued for the duration of the run, the title had been so closely identified with its bizarre lead story that Brown's decision to abruptly shift gears represented a significant creative and financial risk. Always willing to go against expectations and follow his restless imagination, Brown took a gamble that eventually paid off, and he would soon find renewed success and critical acclaim with a bold new artistic direction and a move to a different publisher who was itself in the process of changing the landscape of early 1990s alternative comics.

CHAPTER 3

Autobiographical Disclosures

Short Stories, *The Playboy*, and *I Never Liked You*

When issue 19 of *Yummy Fur* arrived in January 1990, it carried a cover showing a worn shoe stepping on broken glass, on a sidewalk littered with a few autumnal and crumpled-up maple leaves. Ever since the cover of the very first Vortex issue had depicted a headscarf-clad woman looking directly at the reader while asking "darling why are you hiding your gerbils from me?" (*Yummy Fur* #1, 1), Brown had clearly conceived of the covers as extensions of both the comic's nonsensical name and the surrealist premise on which its early issues were based.[1] While subsequent covers typically had an oblique and slightly offbeat relationship to the issue's content—such as a single enlarged panel from the Ed story within or a loose riff on the idea of interdimensional portals—Brown would occasionally create a cover that appeared to have nothing to do with neither Ed nor the Gospel adaptations. As readers came to expect this playful approach, each new cover would help set the tone for a comic book in which unpredictability and narrative absurdity were central features. Though it followed Brown's practice of featuring an image related to the lead story, the decisively commonplace image on the cover of *Yummy Fur*'s issue 19 thereby subtly announced a change of direction for the series. Having ended issue 18 with Josie's death and a large image of burning flames taking up most of the last page, along with a cryptic note that the next issue would feature "something else" (*Yummy Fur* #18, 25), Brown had thoroughly set the stage for a reinvention of what a comic titled *Yummy Fur* could be as the new decade began.

Although the black-and-white bust of the mid-1980s took its toll, the decade had overall been a hugely creative period for alternative comics. Emboldened by the direct market of distribution, which typically catered to a more adult and collector-focused readership, artists as well as publishers and shop owners were enabled to take more creative and financial risks. Together with mail-order catalogues and a growing network of comic conventions, this dynamic and artistically vibrant ecosystem created a kind of renaissance of comics as a form of personal expression, where most people with the desire to make comics could reach an audience.[2] While owing much to the underground comix of the 1960s and 1970s, which as Paul Williams argues first "positioned the comic book as a vehicle for distinctive artistic visions" (17), this new wave (or, indeed, "newave") of alternative comics was characterized by an increased diversity of approaches. Whereas the undergrounds had often focused on narratives driven by countercultural concerns like drug-taking or political satire and had largely eschewed long-form narratives in favor of comedic short strips, the alternative comics boom of the 1980s was a much more varied affair in form as well as content. From publishers of different sizes such as Fantagraphics, Kitchen Sink Press, and Aardvark-Vanaheim came such diverse titles as *Love & Rockets* by the Hernandez brothers, *"Omaha" the Cat Dancer* by Reed Waller and Kate Worley, and *Cerebus* by Dave Sim, which together with countless others, as Brannon Costello and Brian Cremins note, "expanded fans,' publishers,' and artists' notions of what comics could and should be" (12).

One of the most notable developments in the late 1980s alternative comics landscape was a surging interest in creating autobiographical work. Although various forms of autobiography have been part of the medium for nearly its entire history, as Andrew J. Kunka has shown, it was not until the 1970s that underground cartoonists like Justin Green, Aline Kominsky, and Robert Crumb began to use comics to tell substantial and deeply personal stories that often touched on their various insecurities and traumatic memories.[3] In *Binky Brown Meets the Holy Virgin Mary* from 1972, for example, which is generally considered the seminal autobiographical work of this period, Green explored his development of obsessive-compulsive disorder as a result of intense feelings of guilt associated with his sexually repressive Catholic upbringing. Inspired by Green and others, artists like Art Spiegelman and Harvey Pekar soon began creating their own life narratives, but whereas Spiegelman's early work engaged with the legacy of his family's experience in the Holocaust, Pekar's long-running *American Splendor* comic book (thirty-nine issues between 1976 and 2008) took an almost aggressively mundane approach and contained short stories inspired by his everyday life and work as a file clerk in a Cleveland hospital.[4] Inspired by this first wave of comics autobiography, a second wave started to appear in the second half of the 1980s, enabled also by the lower barrier to entry provided by the direct market. Dominated by what Kunka calls an "uncompromising confessional mode" that offered "a sharp alternative to the dominant heroic narratives of mainstream comic books" (47), second-wave autobiographical comics often focused in great detail on the personal flaws of their creators. Most notoriously, Joe Matt's *Peepshow* strips, which began in 1987 and later evolved into a single-author comic book similar to *Yummy Fur*, detailed Matt's obsession with pornography, his excessive cheapness, and his contentious relationship with his girlfriend. Common to both Matt and many others creating similar work was an apparent desire to hold nothing back in the pursuit not only of truth but potentially also a kind of catharsis to be achieved through the unburdening of one's most shameful secrets.[5]

In the summer of 1989, around the same time that Brown was beginning to lose interest in continuing the narrative following Ed the Happy Clown, he encountered Matt's work in the Kitchen Sink anthology comic *Snarf*. Among the topics Matt touches upon in the four one-page strips included are such "pleasures of being human" as "nose picking," "zit popping," and "nail biting," as well as the "TV Shows that Made Me Horny as a Kid" (10, 18). Although he had encountered autobiographical comics before, Brown has described how "the diary approach, combined with what seemed like an intrepid willingness to reveal *everything*, gave [Matt's] work immediacy and impact . . . and were a step forward for personal expression in cartooning" (*Little Man* [2006], 169; emphasis in the original). Another simultaneous influence on Brown was Montreal cartoonist Julie Doucet, whose self-published minicomic *Dirty Plotte* had begun to make waves in the alternative comics world after the first issue was published in September 1988. Doucet's English and French bilingual comics playfully mixed elements of absurdity and the fantastic with an autobiographical approach in which she was the persistent main character, in stories that depicted subjects like sex, menstruation, and bodily mutilation. As Brown recalls, "it was after getting a package of Julie's work in the mail in the summer of 1989 that I decided I *had* to do autobio stuff. That night I worked out a rather clumsy ending to Ed the Happy Clown so that I could start drawing strips about me" (*Little Man* [2006], 169; emphasis in the original).

Brown's first attempt at autobiography was a short story titled "Helder" that took up most of *Yummy Fur*'s nineteenth issue. Aside from a washed-out author photo printed in issue 13, the comic's only previous instances of self-representation had been when Brown drew himself as a rabbit receiving mail in the letter column. As if to announce the change of direction in the most explicit way possible, the very first narrative panel of "Helder" consists of a realistically drawn image of Brown addressing the reader with some basic details about the setting. As Chester the character explains, the story that follows is set in the Toronto rooming house he moved into in 1984 and depicts his interactions with a quarrelsome colodger named Helder. Visually and narratively, "Helder" is told in a restrained, neutral style that is in contrast to both the madcap absurdity of the Ed material and the increasingly loose approach of "Matthew," a four-page section of which rounds out the issue. Focusing on Helder's worsening relationships with Brown and the other lodgers, the lead story depicts a few minor confrontations (one of which includes the broken glass shown on the cover) before ending with Helder disappearing from the house. A straightforward and fairly engaging slice-of-life story in the tradition established by *American Splendor*, "Helder" is notable mostly for being Brown's first attempt at autobiography. Brown admits that he initially "was afraid people would accuse me of being a Pekar ripoff" (qtd. in Juno, 136), and although he later included a few such negative responses in *Yummy Fur*'s letter column, the change of direction was largely well received by his readers.[6]

After a successful first experiment, the following issue saw Brown engaging with autobiography in a more complex way. Featuring a cover that depicts a gallery of characters that includes his friend Kris, fellow cartoonist Seth, and Brown himself, as well as a hand that is in the middle of drawing an image from "Helder," issue 20 announced itself as unambiguously committed to self-representation. The nineteen-page story taking up most of the comic is titled "Showing Helder" and is about Brown's process of creating the previous issue's main narrative. Drawn in a looser and border-less style, the story follows Chester as he discusses various aspects of the in-progress "Helder" with his friends, including several conversations with Kris about how he ought to represent her (figure 3.1). The central issue of the story, however, concerns whether Brown should depict himself as directly addressing the reader outside of a few panels that are visually marked as containing nondiegetic narration. With his friends disagreeing about this point, Brown leaves the question of which advice he eventually followed unanswered, but a reader familiar with "Helder" will immediately recognize that any instances of diegetic direct address had already been edited out of the finished story when it was printed in the previous issue. The two stories together thereby combine into a metatextual and self-reflexive narrative about Brown's artistic development that also highlights the many creative decisions built into the autobiographical process itself.

This impression is further heightened by the contrasting visual styles of the two stories. While Brown initially drew "Showing

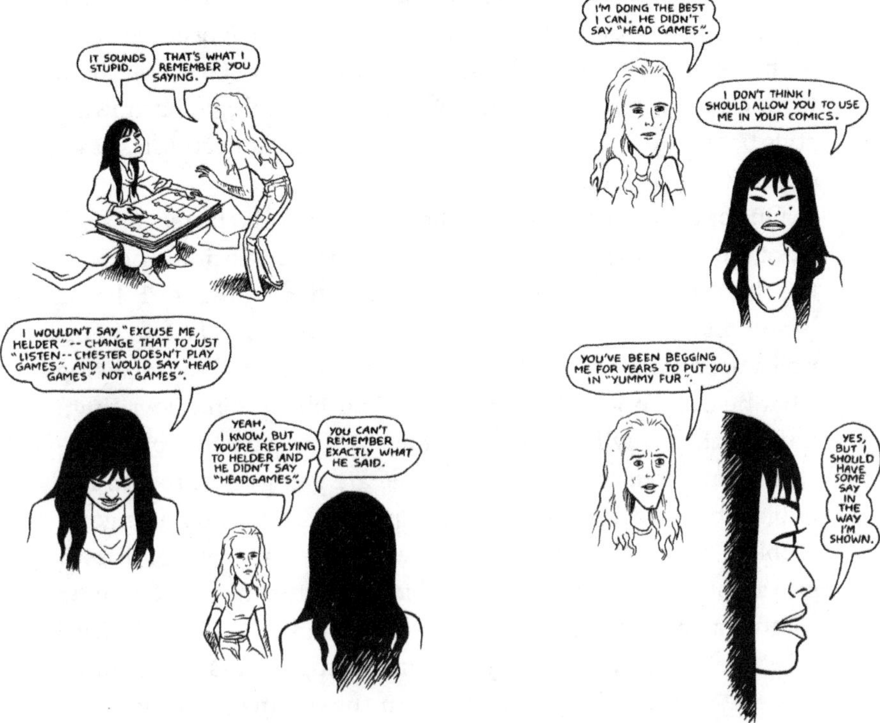

Figure 3.1. Kris offers feedback in "Showing Helder," from *The Little Man* (originally published in *Yummy Fur* #20).

Helder" with the same panel borders familiar from nearly all of his previous work (including "Helder"), he decided to leave them out of the finished ink drawings. As he recalls, "I'd been becoming dissatisfied with my drawing style for a while and wanted it to be freer—more spontaneous" (*Little Man* [2006], 170). As a result of this new perspective, "Showing Helder" also almost fully abandons a standard grid in favor of a loose arrangement of a varying number of panels on each page, a change enabled by Brown's habit of drawing each panel individually before assembling the pages.[7] With only the delicate linework of the characters and a few other central elements of each panel remaining, the resulting pages are dominated by white negative space that visually suggests the dual themes of creative process and the amorphousness of memory. In this view, "Showing Helder" can be seen as a kind of decisive break with the more traditional visual approach of the Ed material, in favor of a significantly pared down and more ambiguous drawing style better suited to representing the various subjectivities associated with autobiography.

One of the main themes of "Showing Helder" is the responsibility of the autobiographer when it comes to representing others. As the character Kris says at a particularly heated moment, "I should have some say in the way I'm shown" (*Yummy Fur* #20, 13). In his notes to the story in *The Little Man*, Brown writes about realizing what he calls "one of the problems of autobiographical writing," namely that "my life-story intersects with other people's life-stories, and sometimes those people are going to think I'm not telling their stories right. If those people are friends, I've got a problem" (*Little Man* [2006], 169). Despite these misgivings, Brown said at the time of his pivot to autobiography that he "just felt more comfortable with the material, certainly more than I would with Ed . . . doing my own life rather than making up this life of someone else" (qtd. in Daly, 54; ellipsis in the original). The solution to this dilemma, Brown has explained, was to set his next story in adolescence, since he had lost touch with everyone he knew during his teenage years.[8] After a couple of short throat-clearing exercises that together examined the potential and limitations of self-representation with stories from his recent past, Brown was ready to take a deep dive into autobiography with his next extended narrative.

Serialized across three installments in *Yummy Fur*, Brown's follow-up to the pairing of "Helder" and "Showing Helder" first appeared under the title "Disgust" in issue 21, published in June 1990. Explicitly inspired by a *Peepshow* diary strip by Matt that details his addiction to pornography, "Disgust" is set in the mid-1970s and tells the story of Brown's adolescent relationship with *Playboy* magazine.[9] Although the narrative changed its name to "The Playboy Stories" in the following two issues (and again to simply *The Playboy* for the 1992 and 2013 book collections), its central theme is Chester's feelings of self-disgust after he repeatedly masturbates to the magazine's playmates.[10] This dynamic is explored through the unusual narrative device of having a small and winged version of Brown himself (humorously identified as a "world famous cartoonist") fly around inside the panels and alternating between commenting on the action, addressing the reader, and tempting Chester the character to buy the magazine. In addition to providing certain particulars about the narrative, such as the time and place of many scenes, the winged version of Brown also functions as a kind of conscience and provides an internal monologue for Chester, who remains nearly silent throughout the story (see figure 6.3 in chapter 6). While it largely focuses on Chester's recurrent pattern of buying and then discarding various issues of *Playboy*, the relatively slight story is brought to thematic life by the construct of the winged narrator, who winks at the reader at particularly fraught moments and overall takes great pleasure in tormenting his younger self. The resulting narrative is marked by a profound tension between the two characters and perspectives, as if to suggest that the adult Brown has decisively left behind any feelings of shame associated with his consumption of pornography.

As indicated by the change of title between the first and second installments, the story was largely improvised. As Brown recalls, "I just started writing and drawing, seeing where my memories would take me. I had no idea how long it would be, I thought I might be able to wrap it up in one issue" (qtd. in Evenson, 108). The result is a story that narratively seems stitched together from a series of separate but vivid memories, an impression that is reinforced by Brown's newly pared-down drawing style and his continued experiments with free-form page layouts. As Barbara Postema argues about the work, "the effect of the loose distribution of the panels across the page . . . is that of an album of photographs," an allusion that "enhances the memoiristic nature of the narrative" (36). This effect is heightened even further by Brown's unusual

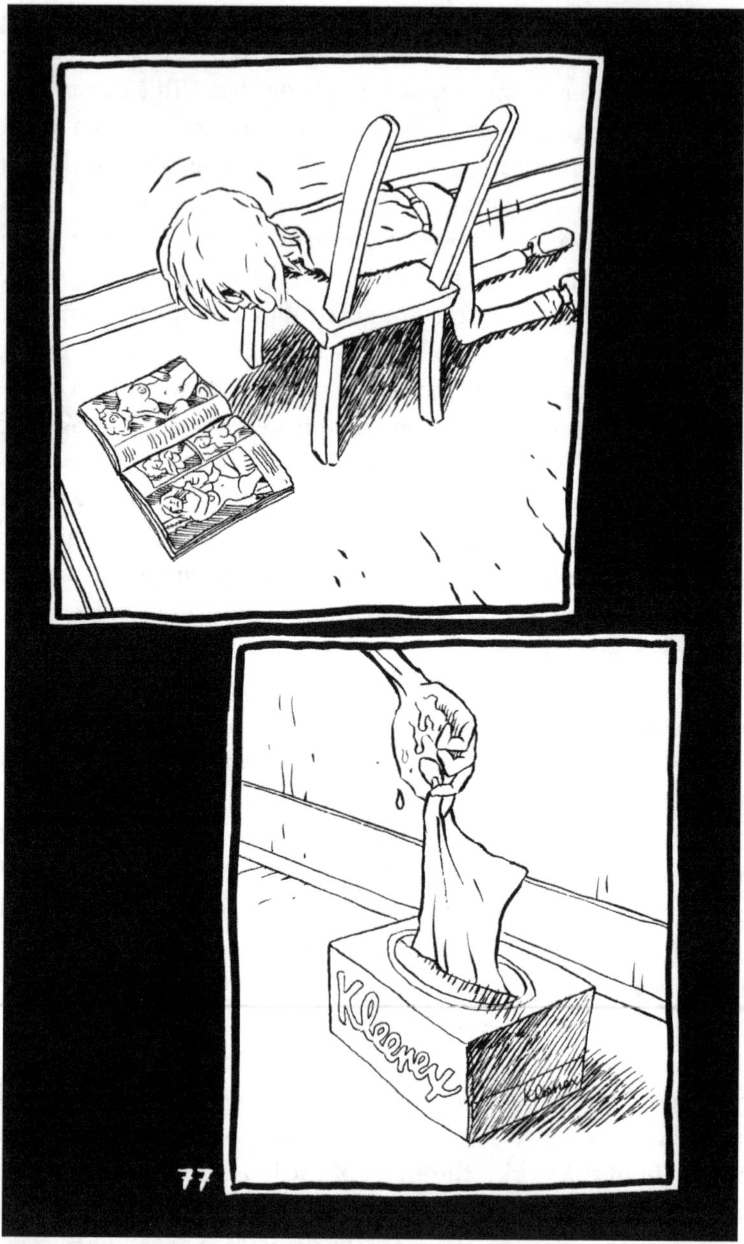

Figure 3.2. Chester masturbates, from *The Playboy* (originally published in *Yummy Fur* #22).

decision to arrange the panels atop a black background for the whole of the story, with the result that the panels have a double border—a black line surrounded by a white line against the black background—that makes each of them stand out and appear as a crystalline moment of remembrance.

Memorably, several of those moments involve Brown depicting his younger self masturbating to the magazine's centerfolds. At the time, these often explicitly drawn sequences attracted significant attention and served to cement *Yummy Fur*'s status as something of a notorious title, since Brown was willing to go further than most other cartoonists when depicting himself in sexual situations. Most famously, the teenage Chester's curious two-handed masturbation technique, performed when lying face-down across a chair while looking at the magazine on the floor, was both puzzling and ripe for parody (figure 3.2).[11] Alongside its boundary-pushing visual explicitness—which in a continuation of Brown's interest in drawing the effects of bodily functions also includes several close-up images of ejaculate—the most intriguing aspect of the story is the stark contrast between the young Chester's intense feelings of self-disgust and the apparent lack of any such emotions by the older Brown. In the notes to the 2013 book edition, Brown explains that "once I published *The Playboy*, most of the guilt and shame I associated with looking at porn disappeared" (*Playboy* [2013], 221), a perspective that suggests that the narrative itself performed a similar function to that of the Gospel adaptations, which had allowed him to work through his difficult relationship with another formative text in a creative and public way.

Although the story had its detractors, most of whom tended to object to the autobiographical approach in general, overall it was well received. Writing in the *Comics Journal*, Frank Young called the *Playboy* storyline a "pivotal work" and argued that it "redefined the autobio genre and opened new arenas for other younger cartoonists" (38).[12] Within a few issues of *Yummy Fur*, Brown's sudden change of direction had paid off, and he was quickly becoming an influential figure in the same second wave of autobiographical comics that had initially inspired him to create such work in the first place.

This second wave was largely associated with the pioneering Montreal publisher Drawn & Quarterly, who more than any other company was responsible for making autobiography a prominent genre in alternative comics in the early 1990s. Founded by Chris Oliveros in 1990, Drawn & Quarterly was originally conceived as the publisher of an ambitious quarterly anthology comic that aspired to "push comics forward the way *Raw* was doing" and become "the comics counterpart to the *New Yorker* or *Harper's*" (Rogers "A History," 15). Through his work on *Drawn & Quarterly* magazine, Oliveros quickly built lasting relationships with some of the era's most promising alternative cartoonists, many of whom were focusing on autobiographical work. After a few successful issues of the anthology, Oliveros branched out and signed fellow Montrealer Doucet for a professional run of her comic book *Dirty Plotte*, the first issue of which appeared in early 1991. A few months later, Drawn & Quarterly published the first issue of *Palookaville* by Toronto-based cartoonist Seth, who had worked on the Vortex series *Mister X* and had become a friend of Brown's. Matt, an American living in Canada, had contributed several strips to the early issues of the publisher's anthology comic, and by the time his solo title *Peepshow* appeared the following year, Drawn & Quarterly had become almost synonymous with autobiographical comics and several of its artists had formed a tightly knit group of mutual influence.

After Matt moved to Toronto from Montreal in 1990, he soon became friends with Seth and Brown, and the three also began portraying each other in their autobiographical stories. In addition to Brown's depiction of Seth in "Showing Helder," one of the first such instances is in a Matt strip dated "February 20th, 1991," in which he draws himself and Brown visiting Seth in his apartment.[13] As the three became close, many such examples followed, including in Seth's *It's a Good Life, If You Don't Weaken* (originally serialized in *Palookaville* between 1993 and 1996), Matt's *The Poor*

Bastard and *Spent* (serialized in *Peepshow* from 1992 to 1994 and from 1998 to 2006), and Brown's own *Paying for It*. Especially in Matt's early work (and later in *Paying for It*, which mostly takes place around the turn of the century, before Matt left Toronto for Los Angeles), the three are often shown having long and ongoing conversations about topics such as sex, love, and their fondness for old comics.[14] Because of the similarity of approaches and their frequent appearances in each other's work, Bart Beaty suggests that the three formed a loose "Toronto School of autobiographical cartooning" (248) dedicated to exploring "modes of confession and self-criticism" (250). While their work was often presented as straight autobiography, moreover, all three artists were also interested in what Beaty calls "the shifting dynamics involving accuracy and authenticity" (250) and sometimes exaggerated certain elements or experiences for comedic or other effect.[15] Although all three produced autobiographical comics that often focused on the unflattering minutiae of their past and present lives, each artist's approach was slightly different. Where Seth's narratives were marked by a certain nostalgia for the past, Matt reveled in depicting his various neuroses and personal flaws, and Brown aimed for naked emotional honesty when representing formative experiences from his youth.[16]

While Brown became increasingly invested in autobiography through his friendships with Matt and Seth, Vortex's Bill Marks was less excited about the new direction and thought it an ill-matched follow-up to the successful Ed the Happy Clown material that had originally put *Yummy Fur* on the map half a decade earlier. At the same time, Drawn & Quarterly began actively pursuing Brown since, as Oliveros recalls, "the sensibility of the company was much more in line with [Brown's] own sensibility, but also because I felt that his work was out of place at Vortex" (qtd. in Rogers "Comic-Book Manufacturer," 64). With Oliveros offering him a much higher royalty rate than he had previously been receiving, Brown decided to switch publishers. After a final Vortex issue that featured a silly story called "The Little Man" ostensibly set in Brown's childhood but infused with some of the same anything-goes absurdity as the Ed material, the first Drawn & Quarterly issue of *Yummy Fur* was issue 25, published in July 1991.

In addition to a lengthy section of the ongoing adaptation of "Matthew," the main narrative in *Yummy Fur*'s debut as a Drawn & Quarterly comic was the short single-issue narrative "Danny's Story." Once again set in Brown's rooming house and depicting his interactions with a belligerent fellow lodger, the story is mostly notable for its first half, in which Brown portrays himself slowly waking up and engaging in his morning routine while listening to the radio. As nothing of much interest happens—the highlight is when Chester eats his own snot—this section of the narrative represents the pinnacle of Brown's interest in depicting the explicitly mundane and unremarkable (if eating one's snot can indeed be considered unremarkable) (figure 3.3).[17] When the character Danny turns up and begins an aggressive and unwelcome monologue, Chester tries to get rid of him and ends up biting Danny's hand when he uses it to block the doorway. Despite this jarring conclusion to a rather slight and monotonous narrative, "Danny's Story" feels somewhat lacking in urgency and is missing the emotional core of Brown's previous autobiographical engagement with the shame and guilt of his teenage years.

With the next issue of *Yummy Fur*, Brown returned to this more fertile autobiographical ground with his longest narrative yet, a five-issue story titled "Fuck" that was later collected as *I Never Liked You*. This story continues Brown's examination of his adolescent years, with a focus on transgressive and emotionally charged language. The narrative begins with a short prologue set when Brown was nine years old. After Chester explains to the reader that he sometimes swaps out real words for nonsense ones, he answers the door and greets his friend Connie with "I *shit* it was you" (*Yummy Fur* #26, 3; emphasis in the original). Immediately after, Chester's mother appears and grabs him tightly by the shoulders while angrily shouting: "Don't you ever use that word again!

Figure 3.3. Chester eats his own snot in "Danny's Story," from *The Little Man* (originally published in *Yummy Fur* #25).

Do you hear me?!" (*Yummy Fur* #26, 4). Following this powerful opening sequence is a thematically complex story that weaves several narrative strands together to examine Chester's emotional reticence and his often-difficult relationships with his mother, girls, and language itself.

The main section of "Fuck" takes place when Chester is in grade ten and concerns the growing romantic feelings between himself and a few neighborhood girls. These include Connie and her younger sister Carrie who live across the street, as well as Sky who lives next door. While Connie is friends with Chester, Carrie has an obvious crush on him, but he instead develops feelings for Sky. As Chester spends time with all three, the crushes remain largely unarticulated until he suddenly and unexpectedly tells Sky that he loves her. Although she reacts positively, Chester subsequently withdraws and is unable to act on his feelings and develop their relationship further. Upon discovering Chester's feelings for Sky, Carrie first becomes jealous and later angry with him, eventually claiming that she never liked him in the first place. The story ends with Sky approaching Chester to ask him to go to a fair with her, an advance he timidly rejects in favor of mowing the lawn and listening to the new Kiss album. With a focus on Chester's mostly passive relationship with each of the girls, the main strand of the narrative is dominated by the many spoken and unspoken tensions developing from these crushes. In addition, the theme of emotional inarticulateness is paralleled in the narrative's two other strands, both suggested by the prologue. Perhaps as a result of his mother's violent reaction to swear words, Chester develops a reputation at school for refusing to curse, which causes others to goad him on and attempt to trick him into saying "fuck." At home, Chester is similarly reticent with his mother's needs for emotional intimacy, even after she is hospitalized due to deteriorating mental health.[18] In a scene similar to the one in which he declares his feelings to Sky, Chester visits his mother in the hospital and unsuccessfully attempts to gather the courage to tell her that he loves her (figure 3.4). Sometime later, upon learning of her death while visiting his

Figure 3.4. Chester attempts to tell his mother he loves her, from *Yummy Fur* #30 (reprinted in both book editions of *I Never Liked You*).

grandmother, Chester appears strangely unaffected, forcing himself to shed a single tear. While it is not the central focus of the narrative, the mother's illness and death haunts its outskirts, and the story is infused with a sense of guilt about Brown's inability to provide words of comfort in her illness.

As an examination of the power of language to shape our lives and relationships, "Fuck" was Brown's most thematically ambitious and emotionally piercing autobiographical story yet, not least because of his increasingly confident use of a distanced narrative approach and an ever more minimalist visual style. Unlike the *Playboy* story, which at times could seem slightly overdetermined in its use of the winged version of Brown to present an adult perspective on events, Brown almost completely dispensed with a conventional narrative voice for "Fuck." Instead, events are presented neutrally, and although the story's many short scenes are arranged chronologically, there is no authorial justification for either their importance or their relationship to other scenes. This narrative approach is reinforced by Brown's maturing drawing style, which uses thin and emotionally muted lines that reveal little about the interior lives of the characters. Similarly, Brown's continuing use of free-flowing page layouts on black backgrounds again serve to heighten the sense of intimacy through the resemblance of each panel to a faded and loosely arranged snapshot in a half-forgotten photo album. With both story and drawings boiled down to their essential components, the narrative and visual withholding of "Fuck" thereby combine to produce a certain formal frustration that complements the story's thematic concerns with Chester's inability to articulate his emotions. The result is an expertly crafted installment in what James C. Hall calls Brown's sustained engagement with "serial auto-ethnography" (102), through which he recursively engages with the central events and themes that have shaped his adult self. As such, both the *Playboy* story and "Fuck" can also be read as a kind of portrait of the artist as an emotionally withdrawn young man, and both also point forward to themes of intimacy and eroticism that Brown took up again in *Paying for It*, his most recent autobiographical work. Looking backward, similarly, Brown's early-career interest in drawing deliberately distasteful imagery is more clearly seen in the context of the childhood taboo around offensive language that is both thematically centered and provocatively confronted in "Fuck."

Although vital to the story's thematic concerns, the title "Fuck" naturally did not survive when it was repackaged in book format.[19] Retitled *I Never Liked You* and published by Drawn & Quarterly in 1994 (with a revised edition in 2002), the book also carried the descriptive subtitle "A Comic Book," reflecting its origins in the pages of *Yummy Fur*.[20] Similarly, both the second Vortex edition of *Ed the Happy Clown* and the first Drawn & Quarterly edition of *The Playboy*, both of which were published in 1992, announced themselves to their readers as comic books.[21] While later and significantly reformatted editions of Brown's work would largely efface their early histories as serialized comic book narratives, publishing comics in book format was an unusual affair in the early 1990s. As Oliveros remembers, at the time "there were no bookstores interested in carrying comics" (qtd. in Rogers "Comic-Book Manufacturer," 65), so even collected book editions relied on specialist comic shops, which severely limited their potential audiences. After Drawn & Quarterly found success with serialized comic books, *The Playboy* had been the publisher's first book publication, and something of an experiment for the fledgling company.[22] At the same time, Brown himself had begun to experiment with planning out his longer-form narratives with a view to the eventual book collection. While the *Playboy* story had been improvised from issue to issue, Brown recalls how "by the time I was working on *I Never Liked You*, I was much more focused on how the story would work as a graphic novel than in [sic] how the serialized episodes would read individually" (qtd. in Evenson, 107–8). As such, Brown's autobiographical stories are emblematic of a transitional moment in comics history, when the alternative comic books of the 1980s gradually began to give way to the graphic novels of the 1990s. Though Brown's work from this period was a foundational influence on especially the boom of graphic memoirs that would become a major strand of the graphic novel format after the turn of the century, Brown himself was once again about to change direction and embark on his most ambitious project yet.

CHAPTER 4

Transitions

From *Underwater* to *Louis Riel* and the Graphic Novel

After finishing "Fuck," Brown found himself at a crossroads. The autobiographical stories had been generally well received and added to his reputation as a prominent and versatile artist in the world of alternative comics. Similarly, the stories represented a clear artistic maturation for Brown, who no longer relied on absurd narrative twists to achieve his effects. Charles Hatfield, in a 1999 special issue of the *Comics Journal* dedicated to "the 100 best comics of the century" that placed Brown's collected autobiographical output at number thirty-eight, notes about the stories that "Brown subdued the extravagance of his early fantasies in favor of an equally provocative sense of restraint" ("Autobiographical Stories," 67). Despite his increasing reliance on narrative and visual minimalism, Hatfield concludes, "Brown's powers of observation and his ability to conjure an environment in all its specificity are constant and breathtaking" ("Autobiographical Stories" 67). Yet because of the personal detail and emotional precision of the stories, Brown himself had started to feel like he had run out of steam with the material. Brown recalls that as he "was nearing the end I was trying to think about what other autobiographical stories I have to tell that interest me at this point. I couldn't think of any" (qtd. in Solomos, 105). Noting also that "autobiography was beginning to feel a bit confining" (*Little Man* [2006], 171) and that "I wanted to get as far away from myself as possible" (qtd. in Solomos, 111), Brown once again decided to pivot toward the unexpected.

This artistic reorientation was partly inspired by a few changes to Brown's personal life. In late 1992, Brown had begun dating musician Sook-Yin Lee, the lead singer for the alternative Vancouver-based rock band Bob's Your Uncle. The new relationship coincided with Brown finishing work on "Fuck," and he later dedicated the book edition (now titled *I Never Liked You*) to her: "As I was finishing this piece in late 1992 and early 1993 I was obsessively thinking about Sook-Yin, so I'm dedicating this book to her with love" (*I Never* [1994], n.p.). After Brown relocated to Vancouver and moved in with Lee, the relationship also found its way into the pages of *Yummy Fur*. In issue 31, an untitled eleven-page story depicts Sook-Yin scaling the walls of an impenetrable fortress, behind which she finds a spindly and leafless tree.[1] As she rests beside it, the tree gradually transforms into a recognizable Chester, and the story ends with their tender embrace. A preliminary conclusion to the autobiographical material, although in a new register, the slight but sweet story was originally intended as a private Valentine's Day present to Lee, and Brown only published it at the insistence of Seth and Matt.

With the relationship having transformed him from tree to lover, Brown also found himself creatively inspired by Lee. Brown recalls how "once I got involved, I found a whole bunch of new ideas coming to me" (qtd. in Solomos, 115), and after quickly rounding out issue 31 with an installment of "Matthew" and dedicating issue 32 entirely to the ongoing Gospel adaptations, Brown began work on a new project. Although he initially planned to simply serialize the new narrative in the pages of the ongoing *Yummy Fur*, the occasion also presented an opportunity to try something new. For a while, Oliveros had been attempting to convince Brown to change the title of *Yummy Fur*, with the reasoning that the surrealism-inspired title no longer was representative of the comic's content and that it would sell better under another name. Although Brown remembers having "no confidence in this plan" (*Little Man* [2006], 171), he eventually relented and *Yummy Fur* came to an end with its thirty-second issue, published in January 1994. After an unusually long wait between issues, Drawn & Quarterly published the first issue of Brown's follow-up series the following August, titled *Underwater* in reference to the comic's new lead story.

The opening page of the first issue of *Underwater* contains a single small panel on a stark black background. As two medical professionals stand on either side of a character lying on what appears to be an examination table, one of them says: "Oo dew na fie zeeth" (*Underwater* #1, 1). Although visually and thematically suggestive of some of the "Adventures in Science" sequences in *Ed the Happy Clown*, the first image and its nonsensical text is a disorienting introduction to the new series. Over the next few slowly paced pages, it becomes clear that the scene is of a woman giving birth to twins, but the dialogue remains unintelligible and the minimal action is neutrally depicted at an unvarying distance. With little to narratively anchor the reader, the passage is clinical and somewhat disquieting. A few pages in, the medical staff leaves the room, and what follows is a surreal sequence that appears to be the first dream of one of the newborns, reliving its own birth (figure 4.1). After giant hands reach into water to pull the baby from the womb, the next few panels appear to be from the newborn's point of view, with faces and objects blending into each other. Following this opening, the rest of the issue sees the family returning home from the hospital and settling into their new routine, including breastfeeding and bedtime.[2] Whereas the dialogue remains unintelligible throughout the issue, it gradually begins to scatter the occasional English word into what is evidently a made-up language, resulting in characters saying things like "are you turlen shuded ulreethech?" (*Underwater* #1, 16). With no traditional narration and an inconclusive ending that simply shows one of the babies lying in a crib, the issue contains none of Brown's customary notes or lively engagement with readers in his letter column, leaving the enigmatic story to stand entirely on its own.

With a challenging and intentionally bewildering first issue of his retitled comic book, Brown gambled that nearly a decade of *Yummy Fur* had built him an audience devoted enough to follow

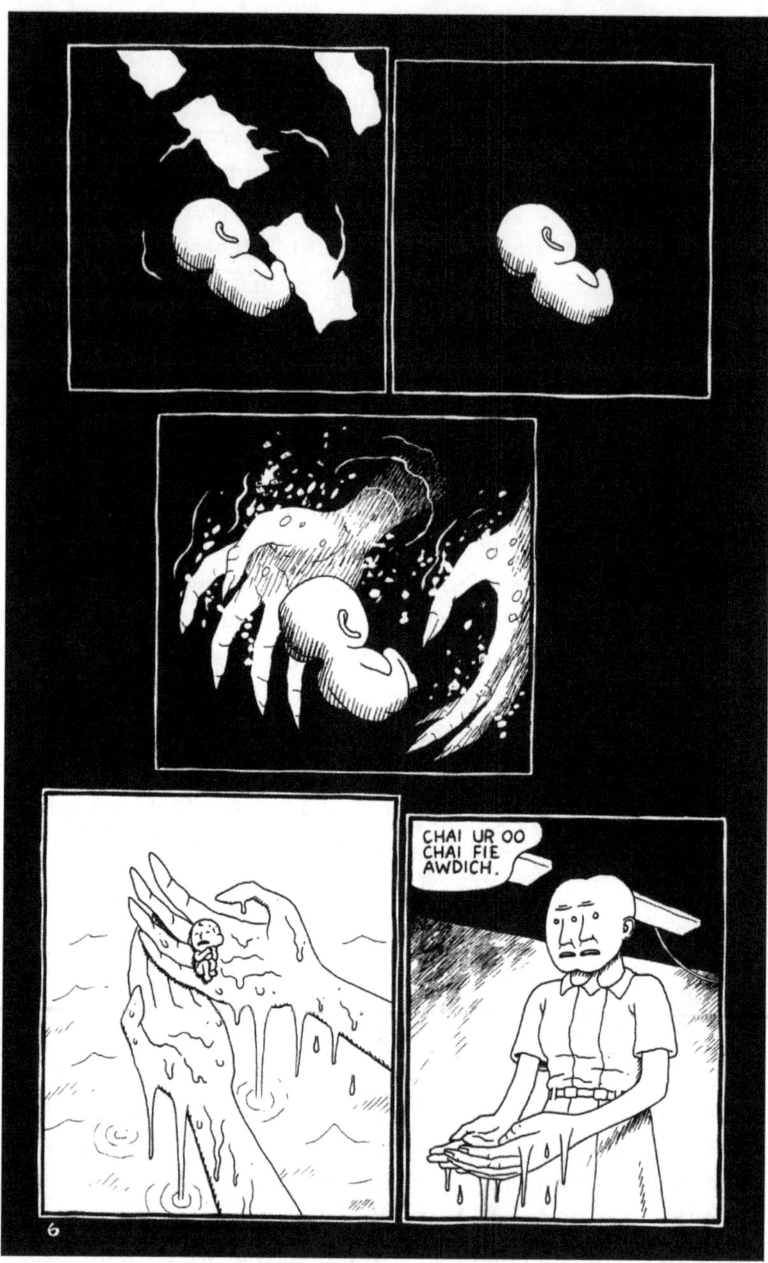

Figure 4.1. A newborn dreams, from *Underwater* #1 (uncollected).

him on any new venture, including one that contained no intelligible dialogue. Although initial responses were puzzled, most seemed intrigued about the radical new direction Brown was taking. Perhaps in order to help his readers make sense of the work, Brown printed several letters with suggested interpretations in issue 2, including a few proposing that both the story and the language was experienced from the point of view of the newborns. As the series continued with regular issues every few months, it became clear that this was indeed Brown's intention, and the narrative slowly followed the mental and physical development of the twins while focusing on their subjective experience of the world around them. Visually, this approach includes several scenes that show the twins struggling to differentiate between external reality and their own dreams or imaginations. Similarly, the made-up dialogue is meant to suggest the aural experience of prelinguistic infants, and it gradually begins to include more English words and phrases as the narrative progresses and the twins begin to acquire language.[3] A few issues in, the story gradually begins to shift its focus to one of the twins, a girl named Kupifam, who continues to learn about the world through her interactions with several other characters for the duration of the series. As such, *Underwater* continued Brown's theme from the autobiographical material of exploring how we become who we are, although this time in a fictional context.

When first conceiving of *Underwater*, Brown was inspired by his reading of the eighteenth-century Chinese novel *Dream of the Red Chamber* by Cao Xueqin. The story of a sentient stone that is reborn in human form in order to experience the pleasures of the world, the novel is known for its scope and ambition, as well as its accounts of dreams. As Brown noted in an interview at the time, the novel "guided a lot of my thinking . . . especially the interplay between the dream world and the 'real' world" (qtd. in Juno, 147). Especially in the early issues of *Underwater*, this interplay is frequently foregrounded, and evocatively drawn sequences inspired by dream logic often blend fluidly into the infants' experience of reality. Visually, this narrative blending of registers is achieved by the further development of Brown's drawing style, which in *Underwater* is even more distanced and austere than it had been in the autobiographical stories (figure 4.2). In developing a visual approach befitting the story's staggering ambition of letting the reader experience the mental development of a young girl in seemingly close to real time, Brown was also inspired by the films of Robert Bresson and the comics of Harold Gray, creator of the long-running *Little Orphan Annie* newspaper strip.[4] Reflecting on Bresson, Brown has frequently noted his appreciation for "the way he kept his characters very unemotional" (qtd. in Tousley, 180) as well as "that stripped-down, bare way of telling a story" (qtd. in Murray, 220).[5] Speaking of Gray, similarly, Brown has said that he was inspired by "his emotional reserve" and "the look of the characters, those blank white eyes" (qtd. in Tousley, 177), both of which are central features of *Underwater*. Adopting these techniques to further advance his already austere approach, Brown also continued his use of black backgrounds and a changeable page layout to arrive at a stark and minimalist narrative that revealed little about the interior lives of its characters.[6]

Intended as a limited story to be serialized across twenty to thirty issues, *Underwater*'s slow pacing began to cause trouble for Brown early on. Although he had planned to write a full script for the story, Brown recalls changing his mind, thinking "oh screw it, I was able to wing it with *Ed the Happy Clown*, I'll do it again with *Underwater*" (qtd. in Epp, 127). Because both the scope and narrative approach were very different from *Ed*, however, making it up on an issue-by-issue basis was far more difficult. As Brown has explained, "at a certain point I realized that, to tell the story I originally wanted to, at the pace I had established in the early installments, 300 issues would be required" (qtd. in Evenson, 125). Brown was not alone in this assessment, and after the initial excitement about the new series died down, its free-flowing form and glacial pace caused both readers and reviewers to express their frustration. As early as in issue 3, Brown printed a letter from a

Figure 4.2. Kupifam eats, from *Underwater* #5 (uncollected).

reader who complains that "it seems to me that these two first chapters have been written with the complete series in mind and avoid the 'quick fix for the reader' element that was previously delivered issue by issue" (qtd. in *Underwater* #3, 27). Similarly, writing in the *Comics Journal* around the time issue 10 was published in June 1997, Robert Boyd begins by calling the series "very exciting" and noting that he "can't wait for it to finish and be collected into a book," before identifying what he perceives to be its central weakness: "If you're going to serialize something, each chapter should at least acknowledge the form—each chapter should be a semiautonomous story unit that picks up from the previous chapter and leads into the next. But *Underwater*'s chapters read like they were cut randomly from a larger narrative" (42). Although Boyd also acknowledges the financial necessity of serializing a longer work in a marketplace not yet geared toward the graphic novel format, the pacing issues and lack of a clear direction meant that *Underwater* suffered from decreasing sales for its entire run.

With a combination of creative problems, a perplexed readership, negative reviews, and poor sales, Brown gradually lost confidence in the material. After moving back to Toronto in 1995 and separating from Lee the following year, Brown forced himself to continue to work on the narrative, but finally decided to abandon it after his father passed away in 1997—an event that, he recalls, "made me not want to waste my time with projects that weren't working out" (qtd. in Tousley, 177). Rather than attempting to conclude the material in an organic way, Brown simply ceased producing new issues, with the result that both *Underwater*'s title story and "Matthew" ended their installments in the eleventh and final issue—published in October 1997—with the broken promise that they would be "continued next issue" (*Underwater* #11, 16, 24). While Brown initially intended to return to the series when he found a way of working with the material, he never did, and he has since described *Underwater* as a "dead project" (qtd. in Murray, 226) that "just kind of confused everyone" (qtd. in Sim "Chester Brown," 186). Despite freely discussing his reasons for abandoning

Underwater, Brown has never revealed where the story might have gone after its last issue, which ends with Kupifam being led to an apartment guarded over by a mysterious spiritual mask, a scene that may represent her formal introduction to organized religion. Today, *Underwater* stands with the Gospel adaptations and the extended Ed storyline as works abandoned midstream when Brown found his attention drifting elsewhere, and like the former (and much of the latter) it has never been collected or reprinted. As such, it is also a transitional work that taught Brown a valuable lesson about the narrative needs of different kinds of works, at a moment in alternative comics history when the industry was itself in the process of abandoning serialized comic books in favor of stand-alone graphic novels.

When viewing Brown's career as a whole, possibly the most lasting legacy of *Underwater* is a short six-page story published in issue four titled "My Mom Was a Schizophrenic" (figure 4.3). While Brown had previously portrayed his mother as a frail and emotionally unstable woman in the autobiographical material, the story curiously does not mention her again after its title. Instead, "My Mom Was a Schizophrenic" is a polemical engagement with the very concept of schizophrenia as an illness, the validity of which Brown and a lineup of talking heads that includes prominent but controversial psychiatrists Thomas Szasz and R. D. Laing mostly refute.[7] After challenging the consensus belief that schizophrenia is a diagnosable mental illness, Brown argues that it is rather a psychedelic state caused by marginalization and alienation from modern society. Using the language famously used by Timothy Leary to describe the circumstances of psychedelic experiences, Brown concludes by asking why most schizophrenics suffer: "Is it because they have an illness, or is it because of the set and setting that this society gives them?" (*Underwater* #4, 6).[8] Despite its unassuming placement as an interlude between the title narrative in *Underwater* and a brief installment of "Matthew," the short story is clearly important to Brown, and while it was not his first time using short comics narratives to make a personal or political

Figure 4.3. First page of "My Mom Was a Schizophrenic," from *Underwater* #4 (reprinted in *The Little Man*).

point, it nevertheless represents something of a turning point in his career.[9] As Brown has explained, "taking all this material that I had read in various books and whatnot and condensing it into a short space" had been "the most fun I'd had doing a comic book for quite a while" (qtd. in Epp, 120).[10] When he later found himself at a creative impasse with the fictional *Underwater*, therefore, Brown began to consider other projects that would enable him to undertake research and engage with real-world issues.

While his work on "My Mom Was a Schizophrenic" provided the initial motivation for yet another change of direction for Brown, the short strip had also abandoned traditional storytelling in favor of its polemical framing. Because longer-form comics, as Brown has noted, "seem to require some level of narrative engagement" (qtd. in Rogers "A John's Gospel," n.p.), he quickly recognized the need for another and more suitable approach for his next project. In this light, turning his attention to historical narrative appeared a logical next step, since, as Brown has pointed out, "history provides you with a story, the story of a person's life, or the story of whatever historical line you're following" (qtd. in Epp, 120). Inspired by his reading of journalist Maggie Siggins's biography of nineteenth-century Canadian Métis leader Louis Riel, Brown found his topic and embarked on the ambitious undertaking of creating what he would eventually come to call "a comic-strip biography" of Riel.[11] Having learned his lesson while working on *Underwater*, Brown this time elected to write a full script before commencing work on the drawings in late 1998.

As he did research and worked on the script for nearly all of 1998, Brown also realized that the ideal publication format for the work was not as an episodic comic book, but as a lengthy standalone graphic novel. While historical biography has appeared as a prominent genre of the comics medium in the last two decades—influenced, in large part, by Brown himself—the market for such work was vanishingly small at the turn of century. With Drawn & Quarterly only securing bookstore distribution in 1997, moreover, and with such distribution only accounting for 5 percent of the company's total sales for the first few years, Oliveros managed to convince Brown to opt for serialization yet again.[12] Reasoning, as Brown recalls, that the individual comic books would provide the narrative with "'market presence' in the comic-book shops," Oliveros also "pointed out that the pamphlets would give me some sort of income while I created the work" (*Louis Riel* [2013], 275). While Brown was ready to leave behind a publication model that had served him well for fifteen years but which was beginning to show its creative and financial limitations, the market itself had yet to catch up and provide a workable framework for the kind of comics he had become increasingly interested in creating.

Following a nearly two-year break in new material from Brown, the first issue of *Louis Riel* finally appeared in June 1999.[13] Noting on the cover that "this is the first of approximately ten comic-books which will tell the true story of this 19th century individual," Brown made clear from the beginning that this new endeavor was envisioned as a limited series. Perhaps to reassure readers familiar with *Underwater*, Brown also noted in a section called "preliminary matters" that he was working from a script indicating that the final work would consist of 214 pages, although "that figure is unreliable—I'll almost certainly be making changes as I draw the strip" (*Louis Riel* #1, 24). Acknowledging that "the series will not be a full biographical treatment of Riel" and that he would be "concentrating mostly on his antagonistic relationship with the Canadian government," Brown also cautioned the reader to expect "distortions reflecting my own biases" and admitted that "it is probably obvious from this first instalment that I believe the Métis cause was just, and that the Canadian government was in the wrong" (*Louis Riel* #1, 24). With the book framed from its beginning as a highly selective and politically motivated engagement with the life of Riel, Brown has later said about the work that he "set out to make the Canadian government look as bad as possible, because my political stance when I began the project was anarchism" (qtd. in Wivel, 160–61). Although Brown had up to this point largely kept his personal politics out of his comics work, that situation was about to drastically change.

A little-known figure in the rest of the world, Louis Riel looms large in the Canadian imaginary. Born in 1844 in what would later become the province of Manitoba, Riel was a political leader of the Métis (a population of mixed French Canadian and Indigenous descent) during two rebellions against the Canadian government in 1869–70 and 1885, the latter of which ultimately led to his execution for treason. As an advocate of the property and political rights of the Métis against the interests of the national government, Riel remains a controversial character in Canadian history, where he has alternately been portrayed as a heroic Indigenous rebel, a French Canadian Catholic martyr, or a traitor to confederation, depending on one's political point of view. In addition, Riel has developed a reputation as something of a mystic, due to alleged religious visions that caused him to believe himself a prophet of the new world. Enshrouded in ambiguity and contradiction, Riel's life story has been told countless times and from many different perspectives. The result, as Andrew Lesk summarizes, is that "Riel has disappeared in favour of whatever contemporary function he might be put to use" (65). As Brown himself has noted, the circumstances of Riel's life have been subject to such varying interpretations that "you can't know the truth at this point" (qtd. in Wivel, 160). Motivated in part by this ambiguity, Brown entered the fray with an ambitious two-hundred-page comics biography that was both highly personal and curiously detached in its portrayal of Riel and his historical context.

In *Louis Riel*, Brown's narrative is grounded in an objective style that portrays events as simply unfolding, with the use of minimal narration and scene-setting. As the various personal and political conflicts develop, Brown focuses on moments of decision and reaction, only occasionally touching upon the personal lives and motivations of Riel and the narrative's other main characters (figure 4.4).[14] In an essay printed in the "tenth anniversary edition" of the book, Sean Rogers argues that "Brown's storytelling

Figure 4.4. Louis Riel confronts federal land surveyors, from *Louis Riel*.

is documentary in the truest sense, merely relaying a state of affairs with little in the way of justification, judgment, or commentary" ("Untitled Afterword," 325). Taking a slightly different view of Brown's highly restricted narrative, Tim Lanzendörfer argues that by "forcing the reader to actively engage in making the story . . . the biography re-emphasizes its own nature as a narrative, and its own readiness for alternative interpretations" (39). This apparently contradictory effect of seeming at once narratively transparent yet highly and obviously constructed is aided by a fully refined visual style that is a further development from Brown's drawings in *Underwater*. Continuously influenced by Gray, Brown draws with a heightened precision and overall visual clarity that turns each panel into a crystalline but emotionally neutral evocation of a single moment. Similarly, Brown's by now well-established practice of following Gray in depicting his characters with blank, open eyes contributes to the overall sense of emotional and visual restraint. Using shadowing and crosshatching only sparingly, Brown mostly draws his characters at a distance and often outdoors against the flat and snowy landscapes of the Canadian prairies, a technique that together with the large white margins contributes to what Lesk calls the comic's overall "planar, austere iconography" (65). Combined with dialogue that is often deliberately stilted and intended to provide exposition, the overall visual and narrative impression of *Louis Riel* is one of artifice, distance, and minimalism.

Emotionally subdued and visually dwarfed by their vast and inhospitable environment, the characters of *Louis Riel* often seem like actors in a story conducted from far away, an approach that also serves to accentuate the comic's central political conflict between the Métis and the geographically distant national government in Ottawa. As Candida Rifkind argues, Brown portrays Riel as "a reluctant hero who favours reason and the political process over violence, but whose fate is shaped by Ottawa's corruption, greed, and racism" (136). A key exception to this outside perspective is when Riel experiences a religious vision and a subsequent mental breakdown that eventually leads to him being committed to an asylum in Montreal. In a striking scene near the midpoint of the narrative, Brown depicts Riel praying on top of a mountain, before being surrounded by fire and floating away into the cosmos. As a visual literalization of Riel's subjective experience, the sequence serves to help the reader identify with his perspective, at the same time that it engages with questions regarding both his sanity and popular accounts thereof.

In contrast to the narrative's overall sympathy for Riel, the comic's antigovernment intentions means that Canadian prime minister John A. Macdonald appears as the story's antagonist, to the point where Brown draws him with a comically large nose to accentuate his villainous duplicity. So committed is Brown to his unfavorable portrayal of Macdonald that he begins the story with a scene set in London, England, in which Macdonald purchases Rupert's Land (a large swath of what is now Canada, including the future Manitoba) from The Hudson's Bay Company, an event that sets the rest of the narrative in motion (see figure 6.4 in chapter 6). As Brown is himself quick to point out in the notes, however, "Macdonald was not in London in March 1869, and did not participate in the negotiations" (*Louis Riel* #1, 24). By nevertheless choosing to portray Macdonald as directly involved, Brown not only personifies the collected actions of the Canadian government in service of his political agenda, he also introduces a dimension of internal ambiguity into the story. In his notes to a later sequence, similarly, in which Macdonald is shown to knowingly send a confrontational telegram that inspired the 1885 rebellion, Brown writes that according to his research, "the choice seems to be between believing that Macdonald abused his power or that the government operated inefficiently" (*Louis Riel* #6, 24). Admitting that "I honestly don't have a strong opinion on the matter one way or the other," Brown says he chose the first (and less conventional) interpretation of events "because it makes Macdonald seem more villainous—villains are fun in a story, and

I'm trying to tell this story in an engaging manner" (*Louis Riel* #6, 24). In *Louis Riel*, Brown's notes are full of such instances, in which he points out the many varying interpretations of events, as well as his own minor and sometimes major inaccuracies or fabrications. As Lesk argues about the comic's built-in epistemological instability, "this metanarrative commentary reveals a contradictory impulse: Brown strongly implies that his comic depiction borders on misrepresentation, though he does nothing to correct the impression" (73). The result is a story that loudly advertises its status as Brown's personal and frequently unconventional interpretation of events, structured for narrative enjoyment and according to an anti-government logic that strongly identifies with Riel's position.[15]

When the tenth and final issue of *Louis Riel* appeared in April 2003, Brown had worked on writing and drawing the narrative for over five years. Although the individual issues had seen declining sales numbers reflective of a diminishing market for serialized comic books, the work was an unexpected but immediate success when it was revised and collected as a graphic novel later that same year.[16] The late 1990s had been a difficult time for both alternative and mainstream comics publishers, but the book edition of *Louis Riel* was part of a new wave of ambitiously conceived graphic novels that aimed for traditional bookstore distribution rather than relying on specialist comics shops. Benefiting also from the prominence of its title character in the Canadian cultural imagination, *Louis Riel* quickly went through printings and within the year had sold more copies than any other Canadian comic before it, and enough to achieve bestseller status twice over.[17] By 2011, the book had sold fifty thousand copies, a figure leading Rifkind to describe it as "a powerhouse of Canadian publishing and a landmark of comics biography" (136). Internationally, too, the book was a success, with translations into French, Spanish, Italian, and Polish.[18] The critical reception was similarly positive, and the book was enthusiastically reviewed in publications ranging from *Time* to the national Canadian newspaper the *Globe and Mail*, while also winning Brown two Harvey Awards for "Best Writer" and "Best Graphic Album of Previously Published Work."

With the graphic novel version of *Louis Riel*, the onetime author of a surrealist and scatological alternative comic book called *Yummy Fur* took a giant step into the cultural mainstream. That Brown did so with a deliberately contradictory narrative that used a distanced visual style and repeatedly announced its own unreliability as historical document across twenty-four pages of handwritten notes is testament both to the strength of his singular vision and the creative accomplishment of the work itself. In the context of Brown's career as a whole, however, *Louis Riel* is not so much a departure as a continuation of several themes and artistic currents that had preoccupied him throughout his career, including questions of religion, sanity, and how we become who we are, told through stark visuals and an increasingly pared-down narrative approach. With its overt politics, *Louis Riel* also points forward to Brown's later work, which would see him abandon fiction in favor of a pair of explicitly polemical narratives for which he returned to autobiography and biblical adaptation, although in an entirely new key.

CHAPTER 5

Prostitution, Politics, and the Bible

Paying for It and *Mary Wept Over the Feet of Jesus*

After the creative and financial success of *Louis Riel*, Brown was in no hurry to begin another large project and instead spent some time revisiting an earlier work. In 2001, while still drawing *Louis Riel*, Brown had come up with a new ending for *Ed the Happy Clown* that he liked better than the one included in the "definitive" edition published by Vortex in 1992.[1] Excited about his new idea, Brown set aside work on *Louis Riel* while he worked on the script. Although he quickly returned to *Louis Riel*, Brown decided to continue playing around with the new Ed material when the time came to begin a new project in early 2004.[2] As Brown has recalled, "that new ending suggested ways that it could be foreshadowed in earlier parts of the story and I began to rewrite some of the earlier scenes. Those changes led to ideas for other changes, and pretty soon I found myself rewriting the whole thing" (*Ed* #9, 23). A few months later, Brown had finished an entirely new script, and since he had also come to dislike most of the artwork in the original narrative, he set about to completely redraw the entire story. Worrying, as he remembers, that "everyone would think I was nuts" (*Ed* #9, 23) for having embarked on such an extensive revision of a comic originally published over a decade earlier, Brown kept the project secret, telling Oliveros that he was merely working on a new ending. Once Oliveros suggested serializing the original narrative but with the new ending, however, Brown admitted to his plans for a total revision and proposed that they serialize the original 1992 narrative, saving the revised version for a later book edition.

As exemplified by the publication history of *Louis Riel*, the market for serialized alternative comic books had declined steeply since the 1980s and early 1990s, but stand-alone graphic novels sold in bookstores appeared as a viable new format for comics publishing in the early 2000s. In that light—and considering Brown's recently increased public profile and respectability as a serious "graphic novelist" engaging with weighty themes from Canadian history—electing to reserialize a decades-old storyline dominated by scatology and narrative absurdity was something of an unexpected follow-up. Consisting of nine issues and published quarterly over the span of about a year and a half, the series was aimed more at longstanding fans used to buying serialized comics than at Brown's newly expanded audience. This was especially so since each issue also included a lengthy notes section providing detailed background and other commentary likely to appeal to readers already familiar with the work.

When the first issue appeared in February 2005, it also included a foreword by Brown in which he described his intention to revise the entire work for a future book, while admitting that "that plan could change if I don't end up liking the new material I'm doing for the story—I've spent several months this year working on that material, and . . . well . . . I'm not sure what I think of it at this point in time" (*Ed* #1, 2; ellipses in the original). By the time the ninth and final issue was published in September 2006, Brown admitted (in a notes section dated October 2005) that despite having penciled around one hundred pages of the new version, he now realized that it "was *not* an improvement over the 1992 version" (*Ed* #9, 24; emphasis in the original). Coming to the conclusion that the two years of work required to finish the project would be better spent working on something else, Brown "put the one-hundred pages that I penciled in 2004 on the shelf, never to be finished" (*Ed* #9, 24).[3] As such, the rewritten and redrawn version of *Ed the Happy Clown* joined the original *Yummy Fur* serialization of the narrative—as well as the Gospel adaptations, *Underwater*, and several of the earliest minicomic short stories—as planned works left unfinished due to a combination of creative problems and loss of interest. In this way doubly abandoned, the Ed material would see its final (at least as of this writing) incarnation in a 2012 hardback edition that reprinted the narrative from the reserialization along with most of Brown's notes for that work.[4]

After setting aside the new version of *Ed the Happy Clown*, Brown once again found inspiration for his next major project in his own life. In 1996, some time after Brown and Lee had moved back to Toronto from Vancouver, Lee ended their romantic relationship. Rather than being emotionally despondent, Brown found himself able to calmly process the breakup. As Brown recalls, for most of his life he had long accepted that "everyone's supposed to have a girlfriend and that's the natural order" (qtd. in Rogers "A John's Gospel," n.p.). In 1994, however, Brown had found his thinking on the matter influenced by the notorious issue 186 of his friend Dave Sim's long-running comic *Cerebus*, in which Sim discusses what he sees as the tendency of women to make decisions based on emotions rather than reasoning. Arguing that the "Emotional Female Void devours what is left of the civilisation which has been built by the Rational Male Light" (*Cerebus* #186, 10–11; capitalization in the original), Sim's obvious misogyny severely and irrevocably damaged his reputation as one of the leading figures of 1980s and 1990s alternative comics.[5] While Brown is quick to point out that he "didn't agree with all the misogynistic views—I didn't agree that women are inferior, all that stuff" (qtd. in Rogers "A John's Gospel," n.p.), the controversial issue of *Cerebus* nevertheless showed him that "you don't have to think like everyone else thinks about these things" (qtd. in Rogers "A John's Gospel," n.p.). While attributing a change in his thinking about relationships to a misogynistic rant in a self-published alternative comic book might at first seem dubious, Brown sincerely reflects that the comic was "one of the reasons why when [Lee] did break up with me, I was able to accept it without being emotionally upset about it" (qtd. in Rogers "A John's Gospel," n.p.). Although their romantic relationship ended, Brown and Lee kept living together in her house until

2001, when Brown moved out and purchased a small condo of his own.[6] In the years after the break-up, Brown enjoyed his status as romantically unattached but missed the sexual dimension of being in a relationship. After a few years of celibacy, in 1999 Brown made the decision to start seeing sex workers.

When it arrived in 2011, Brown's follow-up to *Louis Riel* was a graphic novel called *Paying for It: A Comic-Strip Memoir about Being a John*. As indicated by its subtitle, the book is an autobiographical account of Brown's many years of paying for sex, an arrangement he quickly came to favor over romantic relationships.[7] Brown's original idea had been to do a book covering his entire sex life, from the time of losing his virginity onward, but he had to change his plan after both of his previous girlfriends objected to him portraying their intimate lives together. Deciding to focus only on his relationships with sex workers, Brown this time skipped the serialization step—the readership for which would at this time have been vanishingly small—and began working on a full script for a graphic novel. With *Louis Riel*, Brown had sketched out his script on pages divided into a six-panel grid, but he changed his approach after hearing children's book author Barbara Reid discuss her method of writing using Post-it notes. Realizing that the ability to easily rearrange or add panels at the script stage would be a perfect match for his longstanding technique of drawing each individual panel by itself and assembling the narrative later, Brown spent a year writing the script in this way before commencing work on the drawings.

As the follow-up to the historical biography of *Louis Riel*, the topic of *Paying for It* was both unexpected and controversial for a creator who had recently appeared on multiple bestseller lists and helped establish the graphic novel as a category for serious-minded comics intended for an adult readership. Compared to *The Playboy* and *I Never Liked You*, moreover, both of which were rooted firmly in Brown's past and carried the implication that the adult author had overcome his teenage insecurities and sexual obsessions enough to engage with them artistically, *Paying for It* is a current and direct confrontation with the cultural taboo of prostitution, with Brown himself as its central character. Regarding the change of direction, Brown has mischievously noted that "I take an immature delight in surprising people" (qtd. in McGillis, 216), and when asked about the work's depiction of usually private subject matter has replied by questioning the very concept of personal secrets: "Why do we even have secrets? Why do I care if people know this or that about me?" (qtd. in Köhler, 211). Despite his personal—and unusual—lack of concern about this kind of sexual self-exposure, Brown soon found that the story he wanted to tell differed significantly from the story he was able to tell, given the constraints of writing and drawing about the clandestine and often illegal activities of sex workers.[8] Having initially planned to write extensively about the lives of the sex workers themselves, based on his many conversations with them, Brown instead felt it necessary to create the book strictly from his own somewhat narrow point of view.

Beginning with a scene set in 1996 in which Sook-Yin tells Chester that she is falling in love with someone else, the first few chapters of *Paying for It* traces Brown's gradual decision to give up on romantic love and start paying for sex.[9] Although Chester at first attributes his lack of jealousy to having "conquered something negative within myself," he soon acknowledges that "I've got two competing desires—the desire to have sex, versus the desire to *not* have a girlfriend" (*Paying for It* [2011], 9, 16; emphasis in the original). Realizing that he lacks the necessary social skills for casual sex, Chester is eventually emboldened to seek out escorts after reading a book by sex advice columnist Dan Savage that makes it sound like a simple business transaction. What follows is the book's most humorous section, in which a clueless Chester first cruises around Toronto on his bicycle looking for streetwalkers. When that approach fails to yield results, Chester tries the escort ads in the back of Toronto's free weekly newspaper *Now*, but stops short of contacting anyone because he worries that the police are placing fake ads in order to "flush out the johns" (*Paying for It* [2011], 30). Opting to call from a payphone, Chester's first encounter with a sex worker is depicted in great detail, in which his paranoid imagination leads him to question every step and even look under the bed for hidden dangers. What he discovers is that at least this version of paying for sex is indeed a mostly smooth transaction, and his encounter with "Carla"—who gives her name to the chapter in which she appears—is thoroughly pleasant and satisfying (figure 5.1). As Chester exits the building, a caption reflects that "I felt exhilarated and transformed . . . a burden that I had been carrying since adolescence had disappeared" (*Paying for It* [2011], 48). Although the specific nature of this burden is left somewhat vague in the narrative itself, Brown explains in a note that it refers to his many missed opportunities to interact with women. As he walked out of the brothel, Brown recalls, he realized that "suddenly, sex with beautiful women was easy to get" and that instead of worrying about his social awkwardness he could now look forward to "a future of sexual satisfaction" (*Paying for It* [2011], 263). After this lengthy introductory section, nearly all of the remaining narrative is divided into chapters named after the many sex workers Chester sees, in which each encounter is depicted with attention to its specific context and small details such as his habit of tipping generously. At the end, what appears from Brown's extended portrayal of this segment of Toronto prostitution is an overwhelming sense of normalcy, and Chester's many visits are portrayed as routine and inconspicuous exchanges for both himself and the sex workers.

This normalizing effect is accentuated by Brown's drawing style, which is even more controlled and emotionally neutral than in *Louis Riel*. Brown himself has noted the continued influence of both Robert Bresson and Harold Gray on the book's visuals, but has also mentioned being inspired by golden age outsider cartoonist Fletcher Hanks. Reflecting that Hanks "was probably trying to draw as realistically as he could, but it came out in this very stylized, stiff look, and I was like, 'Wow, that looks so great. That's the way I want to draw,'" Brown has described the drawings in *Paying*

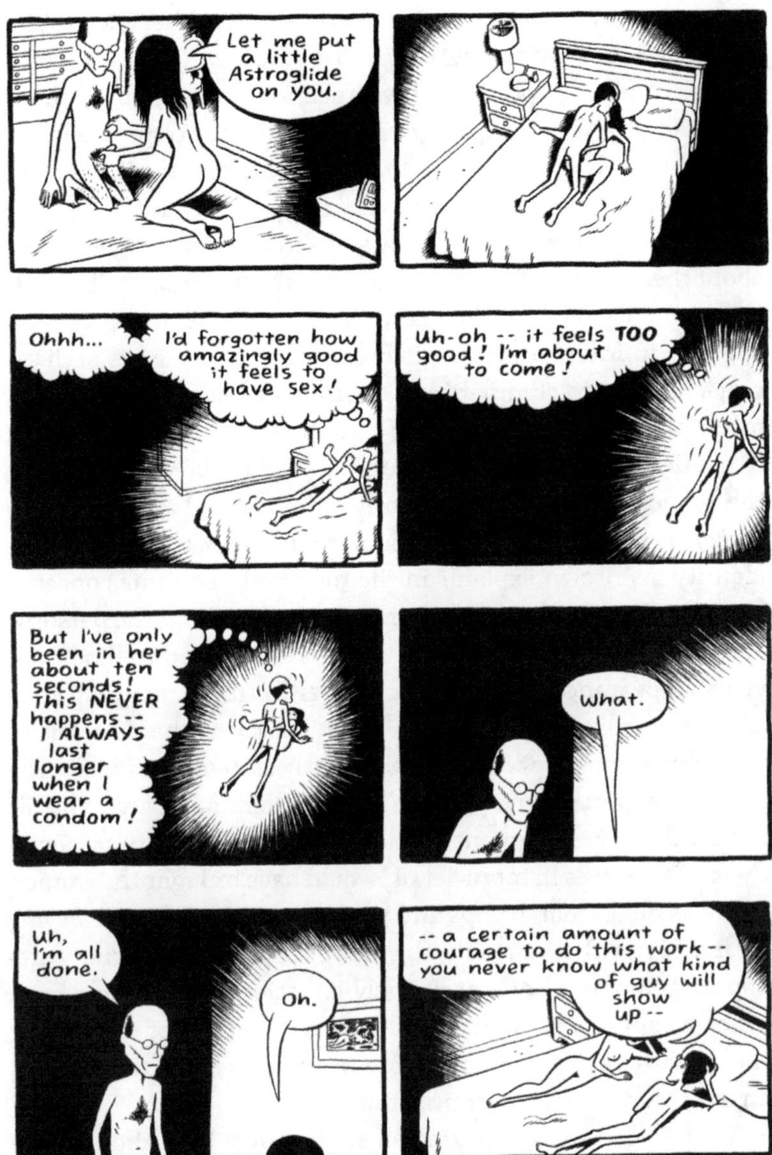

Figure 5.1. Chester's first time paying for sex, from *Paying for It.*

for It as "kind of my style trying to achieve a Fletcher Hanks–like look, but not really coming even close" (qtd. in Rogers "A John's Gospel," n.p.). Composed of tiny panels and arranged in a mostly unvarying eight-panel grid, the result is a series of precisely but dispassionately drawn images that visually mirror the intentional removal of emotion from Chester's sexual encounters.[10] With most characters reduced to a few stylized lines that suggest little about their interior lives, the effect can often appear deliberately monotonous—even in the many, many panels depicting Chester engaged in intercourse—as if Brown is narrowing his stylistic range in order to eliminate any trace of sensationalism from the material.[11] This aspect is further accentuated by Brown's decision to not depict the faces of the many sex workers he visits. Instead, the women's faces are consistently either turned away from the reader or obscured by speech bubbles, in order to conceal their identity. As Brown explains in the foreword, the same concerns about privacy that led him to omit any details about the personal lives of the sex workers means that he also elected to hide their visual appearances. Because he admits to freely changing such aspects as hair styles and skin color, however, the decision to not simply draw the women with slightly altered faces is slightly puzzling, especially given Brown's already minimalist style and his regretful acknowledgment that having had the liberty to depict their private lives in more detail "would have brought the women to life as full human beings and made this a better book" (*Paying for It* [2011], vii). As a result, the many sex workers Chester visits appear anonymous and are largely indistinguishable from each other, an approach that nevertheless has the effect of supporting the narrative's overall strategy of normalizing each encounter as an impersonal business transaction.

The perspective that paying for sex is—or at least should be—nothing more than an unproblematic exchange of goods is part of Brown's larger argument in the book, advanced both in the story itself and in the fifty pages of notes and appendices.[12] In the comics narrative, this argument is advanced in several lengthy scenes that show Chester discussing the ethics of sex work with his friends, including most prominently Seth and Matt (figure 5.2). These sections are themselves deliberate visual echoes of especially Matt's fondness for drawing page after page of the three having endless arguments about sex and comics in the diners and secondhand bookstores of Toronto. Throughout, Brown uses his friends as useful foils for his own rational arguments in favor of the decriminalization of prostitution and against the cultural belief in romantic love as the basis for sexual relationships. Going so far as telling Matt that "the romantic love ideal is actually evil" because "it causes more misery than happiness" (*Paying for It* [2011], 183, 184), Chester's arguments are consistently confrontational and intended, as Brown has admitted, to "wind up my readers" (qtd. in Murray, 224). In the appendices and notes, on the other hand, Brown provides a more measured engagement with the same debates, citing writing by scholars, activists, and sex workers from both sides of the issues, while also taking the time to carefully refute many of the objections he imagines the reader to raise. In appendix 7, for example, titled "Money's Influence," Brown draws an uptight-looking man opining that "money can influence a woman to have sex when she otherwise wouldn't want to," before noting himself that "if that means that the influence of money is bad, then it also means that romantic love is bad. Many people in love relationships have sex they don't want to have" (*Paying for It* [2011], 236). While the book's narrative can be appreciated without reading the lengthy editorial material in the back, the notes and appendices in this way ultimately appear as central to its argument, which is in turn grounded in Brown's by now explicitly libertarian politics based on the sanctity of property rights.

Although Brown identified as an anarchist when he began work on the script for *Louis Riel*, his antigovernment stance had started to find a different expression by the time he finished the book several years later. Crediting his shift in thinking to controversial American journalist Tom Bethell's book *The Noblest Triumph:*

Figure 5.2. Chester discusses his decision to pay for sex with Seth and Joe Matt, from *Paying for It*.

Property and Prosperity through the Ages, Brown has described his thought process in the following way: "Bethell has convinced me that some form of government is necessary to ensure that there are property rights, but I'm coming from anarchist [sic] background, so government should be as small as possible. I guess that means I'm a libertarian" (qtd. in Rogers "A John's Gospel," n.p.).[13] Never one for half measures, Brown started calling himself a libertarian and even ran for office for the Libertarian Party of Canada in two federal elections in 2008 and 2011, receiving fewer than five hundred votes on each occasion.[14] Outlining the libertarian position on paying for sex and sex work, Brown has noted that "people's sex lives, certainly between consenting adults, that's their business, not government's business" (qtd. in Rogers "A John's Gospel," n.p.). In *Paying for It*, Brown's argument about the moral and legal status of prostitution is deeply influenced by his newly staunch libertarian politics, and the book as a whole is an attempt to redefine the exchange of money for sex in terms of commerce rather than morality or criminality.

Part decriminalization advocacy and part polemic against the twin cultural ideals of romantic love and possessive monogamy, *Paying for It* is a truly fascinating book, not least because of its unique combination of comics narrative and extensive supplementary material in the service of an explicit political agenda. That said, the book's most intriguing aspect to all but perhaps the most single-minded libertarian is no doubt Brown's personal narrative of intentionally giving up on romantic love in favor of paying for sex, a position Ummni Khan argues is "decisively queer" (41). As Khan emphasizes, although "Brown is a privileged heterosexual white cis man . . . he is also a sex trade client, a criminal outlaw" whose "desires are queer in their blatant monetization of sex, and in their transgression of compulsory coupling, monogamy and romance" (41). At the book's end, however, in a final chapter set in 2010 and titled "Back to Monogamy," Brown surprises the reader by disclosing that he has exclusively been seeing a sex worker named "Denise" for the past six years, and that she has also been monogamous with him for the last four of those.[15] Challenged by Sook-Yin that he is "in love—romantic love—with Denise," Chester's response is a feeble "nonsense," and the book ends on an unresolved note as Brown comments in the afterword that while he loves Denise and is unsure of how to define his relationship with her, "the significant thing to me is that our relationship should not be against the law. We should be allowed to have sex, and I should be allowed to give her money" (*Paying for It* [2011], 222, 230).[16] In a lengthy critical engagement with the book in the *Comics Journal*, Tim Kreider picks up on Brown's oddly vague conclusion to such a highly polemical work and reads it in the context of Brown's earlier autobiographical material as "the story of a man, deeply hurt as a boy, who resolved never to love or let himself be loved again, and finally ended up falling in love after all, within elaborately circumscribed circumstances of his own devising, the only framework in which he could allow himself to get close to another human being" (512). While Brown himself would likely bristle at such a reading, he has in interviews conceded that despite the book's polemical opposition to romantic love as a framework for structuring sexual relationships, "it feels like a love story to me . . . a type of love story" (qtd. in Köhler, 214). Notwithstanding its unusual format and controversial subject matter, *Paying for It* was mostly well received and further heightened Brown's public profile, with the book also leading to several mainstream media appearances in which he voiced his support for the rights of sex workers and the decriminalization of prostitution.

After the promotional cycle for *Paying for It* ended, Brown once again took some time to revisit earlier work and in 2013 published a revised version of *The Playboy* that completely overhauled that early work in light of his more recent narrative and stylistic preferences.[17] That same year also saw a "tenth anniversary edition" of *Louis Riel* that includes such material as character sketches, pages from the script, and the collected covers from the serialized issues, along with a second notes section. Finally, the 2013 paperback edition of *Paying for It* added ten new pages of notes that engage with some of the book's critics and further explicate Brown's perspective on the relationship between sex work and human trafficking, which he believes to be sensationalized by the media.

As Brown kept busy curating his existing bibliography, he was unsure of what his next project would be. Although he had not intended to do a follow-up of any kind to *Paying for It*, he unexpectedly found his personal interest in prostitution reframed by his extensive reading of biblical scholarship about early Christianity. Inspired once again by Jane Schaberg's *The Illegitimacy of Jesus*, along with John Dominic Crossan's *The Power of Parable* and Yoram Hazony's *The Philosophy of Hebrew Scripture*, as well as several other works, Brown started to piece together an alternative interpretation of several stories from the Bible. Central to Brown's theories was an alternative version of the Parable of the Talents that had appeared in the lost Gospel of the Nazarenes, in which one of three slaves entrusted with their master's money is rewarded for spending it on "whores and flute-players" (qtd. in *Mary Wept*, 176). Similarly, Brown had begun to suspect that the unusual decision of Matthew to include women in his gospel's genealogy was meant to "imply that Jesus's mother had been a prostitute" (*Mary Wept*, 174) in a way that would evade censorship by the church. Sensing a pattern, Brown initially planned to adapt the Nazarene version of the Parable of the Talents as a self-published minicomic, but because this new exegetic framework continued to yield fresh interpretations of several well-known stories, he soon realized that he had found the topic for his next book. Noting that "it seems to me that Christianity is the force behind the opposition to prostitution" and that "the condemnation of sex work and prostitution all comes from there," Brown has also explained about his motivation for the book that "if I want to attack that sort of thinking, why not attack it at the root? Christianity" (qtd. in Brogan, n.p.). Excited about this new project, Brown wrote a full script in January 2014 and began work on the drawings the following April.

Published in 2016, *Mary Wept Over the Feet of Jesus: Prostitution and Religious Obedience in the Bible* is the provisional culmination of Brown's longstanding interest in Christianity and his personal investment in prostitution. Taking him under two years to complete from idea to finished book, Brown has said that he "enjoyed doing this book more than I've enjoyed doing any of the books in the past" (qtd. in Brogan, n.p.). Arriving to the reader in an unusually small and elongated format that evokes a tract or prayer book, *Mary Wept* announces its heretical intentions through a tongue-in-cheek cover design. Featuring a yonic shape with an open book placed at the very top, the main image shows a pair of feet with a few drops of liquid falling onto them, in addition to two snakes among the decorative borders. In light of Brown's reminder in the book's supplementary material that "feet" are often used as a euphemism for the male genitals in the Bible, both the title and cover image of *Mary Wept Over the Feet of Jesus* seem intended to provoke.

True to its descriptive subtitle as "A 'Graphic Novel' Containing Adaptations of Certain Biblical Stories," the main section of the book consists of Brown's retellings of such well-known narratives as Cain and Abel, the Prodigal Son, and the Parable of the Talents, as well as stories featuring the women mentioned in Matthew's genealogy and which portray prostitution (or at least prostitution-adjacent activity) favorably (figure 5.3). Told in an efficient narrative style and arranged on the page in a regular grid of four vertically elongated panels that roughly match the proportions of the book itself, the short stories are drawn in what Charles Hatfield calls "a distillation of Brown's late mode: small, tight, economical drawings, matter-of-fact even when they're mysterious and provoking" ("Review," n.p.). Whereas the influence of Harold Gray had meant that Brown's characters in *Louis Riel* had small heads and often excessively large bodies, the biblical figures in *Mary Wept* appear in almost the exact opposite way, with large heads and smaller bodies, giving them a cartoony and almost toylike appearance.[18] Inspired in different ways by Robert Crumb's adaptation of *The Book of Genesis* from 2009 and Iva Hoth and André LeBlanc's *The Picture Bible*, the latter of which Brown

Figure 5.3. Tamar wants a goat, from *Mary Wept Over the Feet of Jesus*.

first read in serialized comic books as a child, Brown's drawings are detailed yet pared down. Resembling perfect miniatures, the clear and meticulous lines of Brown's panels once again avoid portraying emotion, and the overall effect is one of heightened precision, rationality, and logic, even as the stories themselves retain their mystical and allegorical dimensions.

As a collection of "certain biblical stories," the comics narratives in *Mary Wept* are individually engaging and often thought-provoking adaptations of mostly well-known material. Even more so than in *Paying for It*, however, both Brown's artistic project and critical argument ultimately depend on a lengthy section of supplementary material at the end. Taking up more than a third of the book's total page count, Brown's most imposing such section yet consists of a lengthy afterword and acknowledgments, followed by copious notes (including, in a move that has the potential to make the book never-ending, both notes to the notes and notes to the notes to the notes), a twenty-page comics adaptation of the Book of Job, and a bibliography of more than fifty titles.[19] In every part of all this disparate material, Brown carefully lays out his book's dual arguments that positive references to prostitution in the Bible have been systematically censored by the church over time and that God desires and rewards disobedience from his subjects. Having previously used his Gospel adaptations as a way of exploring his faith, Brown has remained "obsessed with religious matters" and in the book's afterword again identifies as a Christian, although one whose "understanding of the religion has been shaped by reading books that emphasize a more 'mystical' interpretation of the scriptures" (*Mary Wept*, 182, 185). As such, Brown's reasoning often involves obscure and arcane readings of scripture that go against more orthodox understandings, and keeping track of the unfolding argument across the supplementary material can itself be a challenging experience for someone less versed in apocrypha.

The two strands of Brown's argument come together most fluidly in his adaptation of the Prodigal Son, which brings the book's collection of short comics narratives to a close (figure 5.4). After the older brother complains to his father that the younger brother "went off and wasted his inheritance on whores" while he himself stayed home and "did whatever you told me to do. I *obeyed* you," the father replies that "in his disobedience your brother is alive . . . do you think God wants mindless worshippers who can only follow instructions?" (*Mary Wept*, 169, 170; emphasis in the original). Both here and elsewhere in the volume, Brown portrays open defiance as preferable to blind obedience, and the freedom to spend one's money according to one's own desires likewise appears as a major secondary theme. In a potentially incendiary section in which Brown suggests that the anointment of Jesus by Mary of Bethany might have had a sexual component—hence the book's title—he also shows Jesus replying to Judas's objection about the price of the nard used in the ceremony that "it's none of your business how other people spend their money" (*Mary Wept*, 142). At such times, Brown tips his hand not only about his personal motivations for attempting to uncover a proprostitution attitude in early Christianity, but also about his libertarian politics. Squaring his Christian faith with his innate distrust of authority, Brown's personal version of Christianity as expressed in *Mary Wept* is one in which rules are meant to be broken and God looks approvingly upon the unencumbered flow of ideas as well as capital between free agents beholden to no moral laws, especially when it involves paying for sex.

A book of lay biblical scholarship with an explicit personal and political agenda, *Mary Wept Over the Feet of Jesus* is a fascinating but often exhausting work. While the book, as Etelka Lehoczky observes, "brims over with earnest faith and compassion" (n.p.), Brown's selective approach combined with his tendentious interpretations and sometimes contorted reasoning means that the final result frequently seems to be working too hard to impose coherence on both the comics narratives and the larger argument made about them. As Hatfield proposes, "what Brown has done is reconstruct Jesus, and the Bible more generally, in terms of his

Figure 5.4. The Prodigal Son returns, from *Mary Wept Over the Feet of Jesus.*

own political and moral imagination," and the book as a whole is best understood as "a sort of conspiracy theorist's reading of scripture" ("Review," n.p.). A personal and imaginative work of alternative theology, *Mary Wept* represents the tentative conclusion to a career-long engagement with biblical interpretation that reaches all the way back to the Gospel adaptations in the early issues of *Yummy Fur*, in which Brown first used his comics to creatively explore his faith as well as his evolving understanding of its relationship to Christianity itself.

With *Paying for It* and *Mary Wept Over the Feet of Jesus*, Brown all but invented a new format: Long-form comics as political argument aided by extensive notes. Although he said at the time of the publication of *Paying for It* that "I didn't want to drag down the narrative with too much in the way of theory" (qtd. in Köhler, 212–13) and that "I don't expect everyone who reads the book to read the prose sections" (qtd. in McGillis, 215), in *Mary Wept* the supplementary material has become both so lengthy that it threatens to overwhelm the comics narrative itself and so integral to the book's overall purpose that a full appreciation depends on a deep dive into the back matter.[20] The result of Brown's ever-expanding notes sections is the gradual displacement of his work's ostensible subject matter—whether that be the historical figure of Louis Riel, an autobiographical account of paying for sex, or the Bible—in favor of the appearance of Brown's authorial voice and intellect as perhaps the true topic of his mature authorship. With Brown's penchant for revision, it is therefore no surprise that this authorial voice has also repeatedly crept into his early work in an attempt to produce a sense of retroactive continuity around the idea of "Chester Brown."

CHAPTER 6

Retconning Chester Brown

Revisions, Notes, and Authorial Voice

In an article for *Feminist Media Histories* in which he examines the "transmedial paratexts" of social media posts by the cast of the Archie Comics–related television show *Riverdale*, Nicholas E. Miller argues that "it has become nearly impossible to separate the politics of a text from the various actors and paratexts that inform those politics" (205, 208). The result, Miller argues, is that such "paratexts not only inform the present incarnation of *Riverdale*, but also end up speaking back to (and revising) the Archie comics of previous decades" (208). Such "retconning" (the crafting of retroactive continuity through the introduction of new information) of existing material is a familiar trope in the comics world, where the appearance of new characters, perspectives, or storylines often is the occasion for much creative narrative footwork. But as Miller shows, the increased access to readers through various social media platforms means that creators can more easily "craft parasocial relationships with their fans and fan communities" (208) that in turn have the potential to influence how new as well as older work is received and evaluated.

Throughout a four-decade career that has taken him from 1980s minicomics to the contemporary graphic novel, Brown has strategically used the many different paratexts available to him at any time, including letter columns, interviews, an unusual number of notes and appendices, and frequent social media posts, to guide his audience's understanding of his work while simultaneously cultivating a highly specific image of himself. As Brown's career has progressed, he has also continually revisited his earlier work in an ever-increasing proliferation of new editions that have often been partially redrawn, reformatted, or recontextualized with additional notes and other paratextual elements, all of which have combined to slightly alter their impressions. In this process of perpetual revision, Brown's authorial voice has gradually morphed from being largely paratextually expressed to being front and center in the works themselves—in a way, the subtext has grown to become text. The preliminary culmination of this development is Brown's use of the crowdfunding platform Patreon, which enables him to send frequent missives to an audience of paid subscribers. This arrangement is also generative of a heightened sense of intimacy between Brown and his readers through the sharing of such unconventional material as detailed descriptions of his current masturbation practices and various conspiracy theories. The cumulative effect of all this paratextual curation is the establishment of the character of "Chester Brown": A restlessly eccentric intellect who is always ready to engage in debate but also certain to get the last word through an expanded notes section or another lengthy blog post.

From the beginning of his career, Brown has sought out and valued close contact with his readers. Self-publishing the minicomic version of *Yummy Fur* relied on a network of local comics shops and individual subscribers who would receive the comics in the mail directly from Brown. Soon after *Yummy Fur* was picked up by Vortex, Brown introduced a letter column called "The Fur Bag" for issue 6, in which he regularly engaged with readers about various topics related to his comics. Perhaps naturally for a young creator, Brown favored printing letters that expressed admiration for the comic's quirky and often outright perplexing content. A representative letter received from a "C. E. Dinkins" and printed in issue 8, for example, notes that *Yummy Fur* "scalded my brain and left me a whimpering wreck" and suggests that it is "a perfect descendant—and I do say perfect—of those strange, hermetic parables that Franz Kafka and Robert Aickman would challenge readers to extract a meaning from" (*Yummy Fur* #8, 26) (figure 6.1). Such assessments abound in the early iterations of "The Fur Bag," where they function to legitimize and give artistic weight to Brown's creative embrace of surrealist spontaneous creation. By the time of this letter's appearance, Brown had found a way to deploy the principles of surrealism in the service of the longer serial narrative about Ed the Happy Clown. As that storyline gradually grew to incorporate many of the stand-alone pieces first printed years earlier in the self-published minicomics, Brown was able to retroactively impose meaning and continuity upon his prior work while using the paratextual elements available to him in the service of artistic legitimization.

While issue 8 is in many ways a typical early issue of *Yummy Fur* containing back-to-back installments of the Ed the Happy Clown storyline and "Mark," it is also remarkable for including the first instance of Brown providing endnotes to his stories, a practice he later expanded to nearly all his published work (also included in figure 6.1). In a short section after the letter column, Brown points out a few inconsistencies between different Christian texts and irreverently notes that "apparently Mark knew not much more about the geography of Palestine than I do" (*Yummy Fur* #8, 26) in reference to what he perceives as a mistake concerning the distance between the Sea of Galilee and the city of Gerasa.[1] While such comments function to set up Brown as a diligent researcher of biblical matters, the notes section also introduces another dimension of his authorial voice when he admits that "if all of you Biblical [sic] scholars out there keep on your toes you're bound to catch me in a mistake sooner or later" (*Yummy Fur* #8, 26). Although this remark can be read somewhat facetiously—how much overlap does Brown really expect there to be between "biblical scholars" and the readership of a surrealist and intensely scatological alternative comic book?—the sentiment also establishes Brown as willing to admit mistakes and open to being corrected by his readers in a public way. In this very first instance of a notes section, then, Brown puts forth an ethos of intellectual integrity and transparency, attributes issues are still available from Vortex by mail for $2.00 each.

Dear Mr. Brown:
Bear with me; I haven't found it at all easy to deal with YUMMY FUR, which scalded my brain and left me a whimpering wreck when I first plunged, unprepared, into the fifth issue's pages. Progress towards that truly dangerous patch of imaginative ground your work covers has to be fought for.

Getting the back issues made that somewhat easier. Comedy in the early YUMMY FUR was a matter of laughing at death (including, in "Bob Crosby and His Electric TV", brain death) in stories that, looping from absurdity to absurdity to their wickedly pointed end, were as linear as a corkscrew and sharp enough to remain embedded in that portion of my memory where curiosity festers around each radical new piece of art.

You simply decided to pull out all the stops in the Ed the Happy Clown serial beginning in issue 3's "Crime and Punishment". I'm not strong enough to laugh at the grotesquerie you keep hurling my way, not in the context of this story. I do think it's worth the effort of struggling against my inhibitions, though, for weird and cruel and frightening a fantasy as the serial is, it's a perfect descendant -- and I do say perfect -- of those strange, hermetic parables that Franz Kafka and Robert Aickman would challenge readers to extract a meaning from.

As for the Gospel of St. Mark, I can imagine dozens of artists slapping their brows and crying, "Why didn't I think of doing this?" Your Biblical adaptation is a gripping delineation of the conflict of values between Jesus Christ -- the fiery charismatic hero last seen in Ezra Pound's "Ballad of the Goodly Fere" -- and that surly gang of New Testament villains, the arch-conservative Pharisees. You pack more drama and suspense into six or seven pages than most superhero scripters can wring out of twenty three. (Isn't it silly and unfair even to compare them to you? YUMMY FUR is sui generis, but the old habits and perceptions of a longtime comic book fan die hard.)

By the way, I've enclosed a S.A.S.E.; please send me a photocopy of the uncensored page from issue 4's "Forgiven". I am over 21, and offer my appreciation to Bill Marks for his efforts to protect me from the harmful effects of looking at spurting semen. Of course, our delicate sensibilities might've been spared the axe mutilation on the following page, or the bloody knifing at the story's end, over the artist's objections as well; but I'm aware that censorship is a highly subjective art, and that it takes lots and lots of practice to get it right.

Sincerely,
C. E. Dinkins
Oakland, CA

Dear Chester,
Hi! I really enjoy YUMMY FUR; it's by far the best comic coming out these days. Well, LOVE & ROCKETS is great too but I really want to see more surrealism in comics today (I mean, think of the potential, right?) and YF goes beyond my wildest expectations. But I'm sure you've heard all this before.

Although I'm enthralled by the storyline you're weaving, I must add that I think your adaptation of the Gospel of Mark is remarkable. As an undergraduate at the University of Maryland, I took a course on "The New Testament as Literature", and in studying the four Gospels the instructer of our class noted that while John's method focused on the connection between God's omnipotence and Jesus and Matthew's style gave Jesus a more human background, Mark's Gospel was the most mysterious because of the way Mark delineated Christ as a man of actions and few words. Doing much and explaining little.

Isn't that really what any good comic should do? Hmm.

At any rate, I'm glad Vortex has given you the opportunity to publish such a rare treat as YUMMY FUR and I hope more hip people in my area (the Washington, D.C. suburbs -- seat of power, blah, blah, blah) can catch on to your work. I'm doing my part; I work at a comic store nearby, where I get a chance to recommend comics to patrons. Trust me when I tell you YF is top of my list.

Very truly yours,
James A. Wu
Wheaton, Maryland

Notes on MARK

The adaptation this issue covers MARK 6:6 to 7:23

pg. 20 pnl. 5 (MK. 5:1) In this panel (and panel 2) I almost made the mistake of calling Gerasa "Gerasenes"; a mistake equal to calling the country I live in "Canadians". I noticed the error just before YUMMY FUR #7 went to press but if all you Biblical scholars out there keep on your toes you're bound to catch me in a mistake sooner or later. Apparently Mark knew not much more about the geography of Palestine than I do. Here he has Jesus and company sailing across the Sea of Galilee to Gerasa when actually Gerasa is a good 30 miles south-east of that sea. In fact if you whip out your Bible maps you'll see that Gerasa is nowhere near a sea of any kind.

pg. 27 pnl. 3 (MK. 6:17) Mark and Josephus (a first century Jewish historian) are in conflict here. Josephus has Herodias first married not to Herod's half-brother Philip but to another half-brother who was also named Herod; and he has Philip married to Herodias' daughter, Salome.

pg. 28 pnl. 6 (MK. 6:22) Being named as a daughter of Herodias, Salome is popularly believed to have been the girl who dances for Herod.

pg. 32 pnl. 6 (MK. 6:37) MATTHEW 20:2 gives the denarius as the wage for a days work so 200 denarii would be quite a sum.

pg. 35 pnl. 6 (MK. 7:3-4) Lots of Bibles leave out "with the fist" because no one knows what it means. Mark is wrong by the way; ritual washing of the hands was necessary only for the priests in Jesus' day.

pg. 36 pnl. 2 (MK. 7:9-13) I hope you all understand this panel because I don't have room to explain it.

Figure 6.1. A page of "The Fur Bag," from *Yummy Fur* #8.

that would become increasingly central to his authorial persona as his career (and notes sections) developed.

Brown's willingness to revise himself publicly and radically has been one of the defining features of his career and has found expression in countless ways, most of them guided and contextualized by the ever-expanding notes for each new edition of his comics.[2] While the inclusion of notes in a serialized comic book or even a graphic novel is a rather unusual occurrence, Brown has made it something of an authorial signature, to the point where it has become nearly impossible to imagine him dispensing with the practice.[3] Although the notes were initially limited to short sections about "Mark" (and later "Matthew") and appear somewhat sporadically in *Yummy Fur*, they began to take up several pages with the collected book publications of some of the later serialized narratives, before working their way back to new editions of even the earliest comics and eventually expanding to the point where they now threaten to overwhelm Brown's most recent work.

As such, the first two book editions of the Ed the Happy Clown storyline do not contain notes, but when Brown reserialized the "definitive" 1992 version across nine individual issues in 2005 and 2006, they each included lengthy notes sections. These notes were then combined, revised, and extended for a nearly forty-page section at the end of the 2012 book edition, in which Brown also provides the kind of additional material—such as discarded panels and alternate endings—often included in "special editions" of comics and other media. All through, Brown's chatty and intimately handwritten authorial voice provides context and personal reflections, along with comments indicating his shifting worldview and politics. When discussing his decision to include the rat-eating pygmies in the story, for example, Brown first mentions how his initial hesitation was overcome by a commitment to the surrealist premise behind the work, noting that "of *course* dredging up 'The Unconscious' was going to bring some unpleasant stuff to light—maybe some racist stuff, maybe some sexist stuff—who knew what?" (*Ed* [2012], 206; emphasis in the original). After an article at the time criticized him for reinforcing colonial stereotypes, however, Brown initially felt "tremendously guilty" but in the 2012 notes dismisses those feelings by saying that "I now accept Paul Johnson's contention that '"Colonialism" covered such a varied multiplicity of human arrangements that it is doubtful whether it describes anything specific at all'" (*Ed* [2012], 206). In this rhetorical maneuver, Brown not only justifies the inclusion of the pygmies with reference to the logic of spontaneous creation, he also suggests that any criticism leveled against him is unfounded because the concept of colonialism—at least in the eyes of a single white conservative Catholic historian—can be difficult to define.[4]

In notes as well as interviews and blog posts, Brown has frequently and openly discussed his changing political views, including a curious penchant for labeling himself. Although he writes in the 2012 edition of *Ed the Happy Clown* that "in 1987 I was a complete idiot when it came to political matters" (*Ed* [2012], 223), Brown later developed strong political beliefs and has said that he was "a leftist in my twenties, . . . an anarchist in my thirties, and a libertarian in my forties" (qtd. in Murray, 224). In a more recent post on his Patreon page, Brown has said that he is "defining [himself] as an anarcho-capitalist these days, even though I'm not personally a capitalist" ("Pwyll," n.p.). While Brown's tour of the margins of mainstream politics has led him to be a candidate for the Libertarian Party of Canada in two federal elections, his political restlessness has also found its way into the paratextual framing of earlier work. Possibly the most notorious plot point of *Ed the Happy Clown* is the appearance of the head of a miniature Ronald Reagan from another dimension at the tip of Ed's penis. Despite the plot being largely apolitical—though always skeptical of official authority, political and otherwise—in the context of a 1980s black-and-white alternative comic book, such a presence is likely to have been overwhelmingly read satirically and with the implication that Brown was calling the real-life Reagan a "dick." In the 2012 notes, however, Brown goes out of his way to explain that the use of Reagan was largely coincidental and the pragmatic result of needing a figure recognizable to his US audience, before saying that his opinion of the former president has improved to the point where he now thinks that "he's the best president the U-S has had since Calvin Coolidge" (*Ed* [2012], 224).[5] Here, Brown's later editorial additions transform what was once read as counter-cultural political critique into just another feature of the surrealist anything-goes approach as well as a youthful indulgence excused by the fact that he was by his own admission politically a "complete idiot" at the time of the comic's composition. This depoliticizing of the original work through the addition of a highly politicized paratext performs a curious double function by allowing Brown to point out his changing personal politics—with the implication that he has now arrived at a more informed opinion—while simultaneously guiding the reader to understand his earlier work in the context of his most recent beliefs.

Although such subtle political messaging can be found all over Brown's various notes sections, his revisions are not limited to the addition of paratextual material but also include routine changes to the texts themselves. As Brown has restructured, reformatted, and even redrawn much of his earlier work for each new edition, all of this activity has in turn generated its own notes and appendices. For this reason, many of Brown's comics can be difficult to discuss authoritatively since different versions and editions exist of nearly all the originally serialized work from the first half of his career. While *Ed the Happy Clown* has a particularly convoluted publication history, *The Playboy*, *I Never Liked You*, and *Louis Riel* have also been subject to much revision between their various editions.[6] As Brown himself has explained, "if I'm not happy with the initial result, why not try and fix a work if it's being reprinted" (qtd. in Verstappen, 173).[7] This sentiment places him in the company of many other authors who have prepared new editions of earlier work, such as for example Henry James's famous revisions for his collected *New York Edition*. For most comics artists, however, making even small changes to already published work is often a relatively involved matter, since the integrity of both the individual panels and the overall visual page design can be at stake. Thanks to his unusual composition style, however, in which he draws each panel (and frequently also each element in a panel) separately before laying out the page, Brown escapes this difficulty and can easily add and remove panels or otherwise move things around according to his most current preferences.[8]

While most of the revisions between the various editions of the extended storyline concerning Ed the Happy Clown are not at the level of redrawing, the narrative underwent several extensive restructurings between the time when the first short strips featuring the character appeared in Brown's minicomics and his decision to abandon the storyline after the eighteenth issue of *Yummy Fur*.[9] In addition to the question of how to end a narrative that was by its own definition open-ended, this situation presented some practical issues, since at that point the installments of the narrative published in issues 1 through 12 of *Yummy Fur* had already been collected in the 1989 book version. Because Brown eventually came to dislike most of the material from issues 13 to 18, the new and "definitive" edition from 1992 limits itself to the storyline from the earlier book, incorporates most of the sequences from issue 17, and includes a new ending. Alongside the excised material, a lot of which does appear to be somewhat less inspired than the freewheeling material first collected in 1989, the new ending represents the most substantial change, not least because it imposes a moral structure upon a work that had always seemed to revel in being beyond such concerns.

Early in the narrative, when the character Josie is killed by her lover Chet in the middle of intercourse, the scene is presented as a religiously inspired but severely misguided attempt by the latter "to cut off from yourself the thing that is making you sin" (*Yummy Fur* #4, 19). As the story continues, Josie is revived as a vampire before being killed and revived yet again, in what becomes something of a running joke. In the 1989 book, Josie last appears when she kills Chet in an act of revenge, before the story ends by changing its focus back to a sequence featuring Ed and a penis transplant. In the new ending, however, first introduced in the 1992 edition and later reprinted in both the 2005–2006 reserialization and the 2012 "graphic-novel" version, the narrative ends with Josie dying once again, this time by exposure to sunlight, before being reunited with Chet in the flames of hell (figure 6.2). In the annotations to the 2012 edition, Brown explains that his motivation behind the new ending was that "I couldn't let Josie get away with it. I believe that the impulse for revenge is a negative one, and I felt compelled to make her fate reflect that belief" (*Ed* [2012], 243). In the context of a book that began as spontaneous surrealism and arguably overflows with unpunished negative impulses, this is a remarkable authorial revision that recasts the entire narrative as taking place within a recognizable Christian moral universe, alternate dimensions potentially included. Whether the new ending was influenced by Brown's religious upbringing, his adult interest in Christianity, or an innate sense of morality, it retroactively imposes a conventional moral order on a work that had initially appeared to express a truly alternative worldview well beyond simplistic and culturally conservative notions of right and wrong. As such, both the revised ending and the later annotations supporting it represent another example of Brown using the textual and paratextual tools available to him to revise and guide his audience's understanding of both his comics and his current authorial persona.

These two strands would become increasingly interconnected as Brown turned to autobiography with "Disgust" (later "The Playboy Stories") and "Fuck." While focused on his adolescence and as such significantly more controlled than the improvised Ed material, the personal narratives were still composed panel by panel, a technique that has allowed Brown to easily tinker with them for each new edition—a temptation he has been unable to resist. For these stories, Brown originally laid out the images in a loosely organized grid on top of a black background. When the narratives were first collected in book form as *The Playboy* and *I Never Liked You* in 1992 and 1994, Brown extensively revised the page layouts by enlarging

Figure 6.2. Josie and Chet burn in hell, a new ending first introduced in the 1992 book edition of *Ed the Happy Clown*.

and rearranging the images in an even looser manner, while also decreasing the number of panels on many pages. This thorough reformatting had the obvious effect of making each narrative appear substantially longer, and while "Fuck" grew from 118 to 185 pages in the process of becoming *I Never Liked You*, "Disgust" ballooned from 56 to 170 (and again to 198 for the second edition in 2013) in order to become *The Playboy*. In this way, the revisions positioned what had originally been relatively short serialized stories as belonging to the new graphic novel format that was beginning to supplant traditional comic book publishing in the 1990s.[10] Combined with the change in direction from surrealism to autobiography, the adjustments made to the formatting can also be seen as a conscious attempt by Brown to establish himself as the creator of a different and more prestigious kind of comic, namely the book-length graphic memoir.

Crude length, however, is not the only effect of Brown's reformatting of these early narratives. Especially noticeable is the change in pacing created by having fewer, larger images on each page, an approach that slows down the stories and renders them even more evocative of distant childhood memories. This aesthetic in turn creates a heightened sense of intimacy with Chester the character as the narratives morph from comic book serializations to graphic novels. For the *Playboy* story, this intimacy is further amplified by the winged narrator, who zooms around the pages while commenting on the action. In both the *Yummy Fur* version and the 1992 book edition of *The Playboy*, this winged narrator is more devil than angel (as suggested also by his bat-like wings), and in especially the first half of the story he constantly tempts Chester with thoughts of the magazine. The effect is to make each moment depicted seem urgently dominated by an unwinnable struggle against Chester's own shameful desires.

For the revised 2013 edition, Brown made a litany of changes that significantly altered both the visual expression and the emotional tone of the book. The most immediately obvious differences are the exchange of the black backgrounds for white, an increased standardization of the panel sizes and layouts, and a change of overall publication format that reduces the surface area of each page to nearly half that of the earlier book.[11] In addition, Brown redrew parts of nearly every panel—including moving the previously panel-breaking speech bubbles into the panels in an orderly fashion—and relettered the entire narrative in a more standardized way reminiscent of his later, more measured work. As a result of all this tinkering, the new version leaves a significantly calmer and more austere impression, and the images seem more like the carefully crafted miniatures of *Paying for It* and *Mary Wept Over the Feet of Jesus* than the haphazardly organized and emotionally raw snapshots of the original. Finally, panels have been removed, sections have been reorganized, and much of the dialogue has been rewritten, including that of the winged narrator who now no longer addresses Chester directly with taunts and temptations. Instead, the previously unruly and panel-breaking creature has become a somewhat tamer version of himself, who now stays inside the panel borders (several of which have been redrawn to contain him) and only speaks when commenting on the action in the first person, a change that serves to conflate him with the teenage Chester and remove much of the tension between the two characters established in the previous editions.

A representative example of most of these revisions is when Chester fails to get aroused by the Black playmate in an issue of the magazine he has smuggled home from the convenience store. In both the original *Yummy Fur* version and the 1992 book, the winged narrator sneers at Chester that "this is the first time in your life that you've had to face the fact that at some level you're a racist" (*Playboy* [1992], 44). In the revised 2013 edition, however, his facial expression has been significantly toned down and the dialogue changed to indicate that the incident "leads me to accuse myself of being a racist, which leads to more disgust with myself" (*Playboy* [2013], 46) (figure 6.3). Gone as well is the narrator's original taunt of "if only you'd never bought the damn thing, eh?" (*Playboy* [1992], 44). In addition to being significantly less confrontational,

Figure 6.3. The winged narrator assesses the postmasturbation scene differently in the 1992 and 2013 book editions of *The Playboy*.

the new panel thereby changes the meaning from Brown facing an unpleasant reality about himself to merely containing a detached statement about how he accused himself of being a racist, which is in turn understood as a byproduct of the shame associated with masturbation.[12] Throughout, the new edition relies on such visual and textual edits to subtly alter the narrative, and the result is a loss of immediacy as the book becomes less an immersive narrative about Chester experiencing shame than a retrospective narrative about how Brown the narrator *used* to experience shame before outgrowing such emotions. As Brown says in the notes to the 2013 edition, "for most of my life I felt self-loathing after masturbating. That feeling has gone away in recent years, even though I still climax-by-myself most days" (*Playboy* [2013], 213). This change in perspective can therefore be understood as a direct effect of Brown's maturation in the twenty-three years between the first serialization of the story in *Yummy Fur* and the second book edition.

While Brown's twenty pages of notes to the 2013 edition of *The Playboy* do admit to "some changes" (*Playboy* [2013], 205) and—in a gesture toward full transparency—include every panel removed from the previous version, there is no mention of either his significant redrawing or of many other meaningful changes, such as substituting the word "girl" for the more appropriate (for a man now in his fifties) "woman" when referring to the magazine's playmates.[13] Although Brown's ethos of transparency in this way does compel him to point out that the new edition has been somewhat edited, there is no indication outside of the notes section that the work has been substantially and meaningfully changed since the original publication, and the final (significantly altered) panel's hand-drawn date stamp still places its creation in 1990. The overall effect of this extensive editorial work is the retroactive maturation of both the narrative itself and the twenty-something creator of the original comic, bringing both in line with Brown's current 2013 worldview and artistic preferences while effacing certain aspects of his earlier, more visually unrestrained and thematically ambiguous work.[14]

Although "Fuck" changed its name to *I Never Liked You* in its journey from alternative comic book to graphic novel, it has so far been subject to far fewer changes than its predecessor. Originally serialized from 1991 to 1993, the story underwent the layout changes outlined above for its first book edition in 1994, which also omitted a few introductory panels and narrative captions.[15] With the second edition from 2002, Brown reformatted the book with white backgrounds in the same manner as the 2013 edition of *The Playboy* and added a modest two pages of notes explaining where certain events took place. As a result of this comparatively small amount of editorial and annotative work, the narrative makes a relatively consistent impression across the three versions, and the fact that no new edition has been published for more than two decades perhaps indicates that Brown is content with the book and sees no need to redraw or otherwise update it.

Following the end of *Yummy Fur*, Brown's abandoned series *Underwater* has never been collected or revised, and Brown has said that he is "spending zero creative-time" thinking about it (qtd. in Bagge, n.p.). The Gospel adaptations "Mark" and "Matthew," similarly, are only available in their original publication contexts of *Yummy Fur* and *Underwater*, and Brown lost interest in revisiting them long ago. *Louis Riel*, on the other hand, has seen both revision and several different editions on its path to becoming Brown's most well-known and celebrated work. Since Brown worked from a full script from the beginning, the narrative of *Louis Riel* is tighter and more controlled than any of his previous comics, but the half decade spent drawing it meant that his drawing style changed somewhat over the course of the serialization. As Brown became increasingly inspired by Harold Gray, several of his characters gradually developed larger bodies and ever-smaller heads. While stylistic variation over time is a commonplace in serialized comics, Brown's conceptualization of the narrative as a contained work ultimately destined for the graphic novel format meant that he decided to redraw several of the story's main characters—including Riel himself, as well as the story's villain, Canadian Prime Minister John A. Macdonald—for the first seventy-nine of the collected edition's 241 pages (figure 6.4).[16]

Such extensive redrawing in the service of visual consistency is an understandable impulse, but it is not the only option for works with publication histories spanning several years. As Daniel Marrone argues about the collected version of *Clyde Fans* by Brown's longtime friend Seth (which was begun in 1997 but not completed until a mammoth book collection in 2019), "the change in drawing style . . . testifies to the passage of time—'real' extra-literary time" (qtd. in Editors, n.p.). This highly noticeable change, Marrone suggests, is central to the book's sense of temporality and emotional

Figure 6.4. John A. Macdonald buys Rupert's Land, comparison of the serialized version and the book edition of *Louis Riel*.

impact. In contrast, Sean Carney argues about the graphic novel version of *Louis Riel* that "what is effaced here is the *process* of creating the comic book itself, originally seen in those traces of a style in transformation. We might say that its history of production has been purged" (194; emphasis in the original). Carney perceives this effacing of the work's production history through the standardization of the drawing style as part of a larger strategy of legitimization, which sees the comic pass from serialized comic book into the rarified realm of bookstore-ready graphic novel: "in becoming literature, removed are . . . the messy details of the process of artistic creation itself" (195). While editorials and letter columns earlier in Brown's career—when he was still the creator of a surrealist alternative comic book—served the purpose of guiding his readers' understanding of his work, such paratextual ephemera had by the collected 2003 edition of *Louis Riel* been replaced by a lengthy notes section, an extensive bibliography, and an index worthy of historical biography.

Although the main comics narratives of *Paying for It* and *Mary Wept Over the Feet of Jesus* have yet to see revision, Brown has continued to influence perceptions of both his work and himself for a dedicated group of readers through his current use of the crowdfunding platform Patreon.[17] Patreon is part of a group of platforms allowing fans to support their favorite artists and other content producers through a paid subscription model, but where sites such as OnlyFans, Cameo, and SubStack are commonly used by producers to sell exclusive access to their work, Patreon tends to be less content-driven. As Lee Hair argues, the dynamics of Patreon instead "encourages creators to foster intimate relationships with fans" (198) in a way that is reminiscent of traditional patronage. Because work published on Patreon is only rarely produced solely for patrons, much of the appeal for supporters lies in what Hair calls "socially intimate rewards" that require artists to perform "parasocial relational work" (197) in order to gain and maintain financial support in the form of monthly pledges. As a generator of intimacy between artist and fan, Patreon thus has something in common with the traditional letter columns of serialized comic books (such as "The Fur Bag" in *Yummy Fur*) as well as with comics in general—which, as Carney argues, are often "constructed as a form of correspondence, offering the illusion of a private communiqué between artist(s) and reader(s)" (193).[18] For these reasons, it is no surprise that Brown has seized upon the platform as a well-suited vehicle for eliciting financial support in exchange for various updates about his life and work.

While Brown's number of supporters and total amount of monthly pledges are relatively low, the site does offer him a reliable source of monthly income and the setup has also worked to support his inclination for sharing personal details and portraying himself as something of an intellectual rebel to his most devoted core of readers.[19] In regular blogposts delivered directly to the email inboxes of his patrons, Brown has rarely limited himself to sharing such predictable content as work in progress or early sketches from his previously published comics. Instead, patrons have come to expect a heterogenous mix of content that among many other things has included Brown's responses to reviews of his work, his evaluations of various dystopian novels compared to the present day, considerations of the nature of substance addiction, lengthy refutations of media stories about sex trafficking, drawings attempting to debunk the theory of the supercontinent Pangaea, a close-up picture of his damaged penis after an especially rough masturbation session, and various conspiracy theories about topics ranging from the Shakespeare authorship question and the guilt of convicted high-profile sex offender Jerry Sandusky to the existence of COVID-19. In the context of traditional social media, many of these views would instantly be seized upon by other users and dismissed as either deliberate trolling or the misguided beliefs of a (presumably) right-wing crank, but because the dispatches are shared only with paying supporters, the replies and comments on the site itself are typically either supportive or inquisitive. The main exception has been Brown's posts about the COVID-19 pandemic, which he first believed to be made up and later suggested had been exaggerated by governments as an excuse to grab and consolidate power.[20] When a few patrons objected to this perspective, Brown politely replied that "I think having one's ideas challenged is a good thing" before noting that "questioning everything and coming to unorthodox conclusions, that's my path." In a self-conscious but winking acknowledgment of the eccentricity of many of his beliefs, Brown also asked a final rhetorical question: "Do you really want a Chester Brown who goes along with the herd?" ("My Response," n.p.).

The answer, of course, is no. Brown has spent the entirety of his career creating comics that are aesthetically and politically challenging, while also deploying a variety of paratextual material to project a certain image of himself as someone willing to contest any and all orthodoxies. Expecting anything else would be a fool's errand. Through his many revisions to early work and an abundance of notes and other paratexts, Brown has worked against theories of readerly production of meaning in deliberate attempts to control both the reception of his comics narratives and their relationship with himself. As such, his persona and his comics engage in a feedback loop with each other, in which books written decades ago come to support his current beliefs, at the same time that those beliefs retroactively serve to influence our readings of the books themselves through Brown's repeated tinkering with the art and the continual addition of supplementary material. The result is an ever-increasing cohesion of Brown's authorial persona that gradually irons out any inconsistencies in order to offer us the character of "Chester Brown"—a kind of retconned version of himself as a scholarly but renegade nonconformist. Viewed that way, the entirety of Brown's oeuvre—including both paratexts and Patreon—can be understood autobiographically and as a virtuosic performance of a self in constant motion. Through this performance, Brown is forcing us to play catch-up with both this self and his changing sense of what his comics mean and represent, through the implicit suggestion that his earlier work and younger self is in perpetual need of correction by his most current incarnation.

Against the Grain

When Brown published "My Mom Was a Schizophrenic" in issue 4 of *Underwater* in 1995, it was both a central moment and something of a turning point in his authorship (see figure 4.3 in chapter 4). Consisting mostly of a series of talking heads questioning the validity of schizophrenia as a medical condition and diagnosis, the significance of the initially unassuming short story to Brown's most lasting preoccupations looms large when viewed in the context of his career as a whole, in ways that reach both forward and back from this critical engagement with the affliction that took his mother's life when he was a teenager. Despite its brief, title-only reference to Brown's mother, the story provides crucial context for the depiction of his strained relationship with her in his early autobiographical work, in which she appears as a frail and often difficult figure yearning for her son to express his love for her. In addition to reframing both that portrayal and his own inability to meet her desire in the context of a schizophrenia diagnosis, Brown's reference to the maternal relationship also suggests a new dimension to his depiction of his mother's religiously motivated speech regulation, which in turn is evocative of both his teenage inhibitions and the potent mix of anything-goes scatology and restrained Gospel adaptations that characterized the early issues of *Yummy Fur*. Similarly, the confidence with which the short story presents both its challenge to established dogma and its support of contrarian fringe theories—as well as its reliance on a lengthy notes section for context and further editorializing—prefigures Brown's late-career turn away from fiction in favor of politically motivated historical biography, advocacy, and didacticism.

In a 1993 *Comics Journal* profile of Brown written by Bob Levin, Brown declared: "I create out of two emotions mainly. Outrage and Guilt" (47). While "My Mom Was a Schizophrenic" productively incorporates the two, it is maybe only a slight oversimplification to suggest that the first half of Brown's authorship was more inspired by a sense of guilt, while his more mature work has been firmly in the outrage camp. In nearly all his published work, however, Brown's most consistent theme has been a profound skepticism of any and all authority. Early in his career, this antiauthoritarian streak mainly found expression in his depictions of doctors, scientists, and vaguely defined politicians abusing their various powers in the absurd and morally ambiguous universe inhabited by Ed the Happy Clown, but the perspective also came to infuse his portrayal of Jesus, who gradually morphed from beatific holy man to rebellious prophet over the course of the Gospel adaptations. By the time of the earliest autobiographical material, Brown turned to an examination of his teenage years in light of what he saw as arbitrary cultural and familial taboos concerning pornography and profanity, along with their capacity to induce intense feelings of shame and guilt. Because Brown's return to fiction with *Underwater* was ultimately left unfinished—in fact, he has never decisively finished an extended fictional narrative—it can be difficult to evaluate, but here as well as in its follow-up *Louis Riel*, Brown again explored how people become who they are against the background of their specific cultural and political contexts. In *Underwater*, that examination once again took place within a domestic setting, while Brown in *Louis Riel* broadened his perspective to include key events in Canadian history as well as the politics of confederation itself. In Louis Riel, Brown found a congenial protagonist for not only his antigovernment politics but also his continuing preoccupation with the individual's experience of religion, explored through Riel's mystic visions and self-proclaimed status as a prophet of the new world. With Brown's most recent work, his anti-authority disposition and distrust of government have grown to take center stage in renewed engagements with autobiography and biblical adaptation, this time in the highly specific context of the political and cultural taboos around prostitution and expressed through ever-lengthening paratextual material such as notes and appendices (as well as, of course, notes to the appendices).

Throughout his decades of personal and often idiosyncratic comics-making, Brown has also been at the center of many of the developments that have characterized the comics world since the early 1980s. From his years of selling self-published minicomics on consignment, through the alternative comics boom (and eventual bust) enabled by the direct market, to the development of memoir and historical biography as leading genres of the modern graphic novel, Brown's work has been influential to generations of cartoonists. In her history of alternative comics in Canada, cartoonist Fiona Smyth recollects stumbling upon a minicomic issue of *Yummy Fur* in a Toronto bookstore in the mid-1980s, an event that "introduced me to a whole new world" and "opened the door for me to self-publishing" (147). From this generative moment, Smyth outlines the importance of Brown's work to the development of personal and adult-oriented comics in Canada. This straight line of influence can easily be extended internationally, especially when it comes to the appearance of the stand-alone graphic novel as a viable publishing category in the English-speaking world, a format Brown helped pioneer artistically while his publisher Drawn & Quarterly worked to establish it as the financial backbone of twenty-first-century comics publishing.

When he was inducted into the Canadian Comic Book Hall of Fame at the 2011 Joe Shuster Awards, the accompanying text by the selection committee referred to Brown as "controversial and determined . . . an artist like no other" (n.p.). As the winner and nominee, also, of several Harvey and Ignatz Awards, as well as the subject of a 2013–2014 exhibition at the Art Gallery of Ontario titled "Chester Brown and Louis Riel," Brown is a celebrated and leading figure in the contemporary Canadian and international comics worlds.[1] To his friend and cartoonist colleague Seth, moreover, Brown is both "a genius" (qtd. in Dylan Williams, 24) and "the guy who first made me see the endless possibilities in comic storytelling" (qtd. in Groth, 81). For over four decades of frequently transgressive comics-making, Brown has stubbornly worked against the grain to expand the established boundaries of the form in a varied and uncompromising body of work that consistently seeks to surprise, challenge, and—increasingly—educate his readers.

NOTES

INTRODUCTION

1. Throughout his career but especially in his later works, Brown has adopted an unusual approach to hyphenation that in addition to "toilet-paper" and "graphic-novel" in the examples quoted from this strip also includes such examples as "T-V," "U-S," "K-F-C," and "A-M"/"P-M." For accuracy, I have retained these and other idiosyncrasies in my quotes from Brown's work both here and in the rest of this book, dispensing also with the customary "[sic]" in most instances.

2. In order to distinguish between the real-life author and the self-representational character, I will generally refer to the former as "Brown" and the latter as "Chester" in my discussion of Brown's autobiographical work throughout this book.

3. In 1980, the publication category of the "graphic novel" was not yet well-established, and Brown himself is quick to explain the anachronism in his notes to the story: "What I was actually planning was an open-ended series of comic-books. (Both are long works, the difference is that the creator of a graphic-novel intends to finish it)" (*Little Man* [2006], 161).

4. *Louis Riel* was first serialized in ten comic book issues between 1999 and 2003, but as I discuss in chapter 4, Brown conceived the narrative to fit the emerging graphic novel format from the beginning and only agreed to its initial serialization at the suggestion of his publisher.

5. In contrast to the often contentious and obstinate persona expressed through his comics, in person Brown comes across as introspective and soft-spoken.

6. Another memorable example of Brown's rare work for hire is a short story serialized across six installments in Toronto's weekly newspaper *Now* in 2007. A love story following a zombie and a human woman as they go on various dates around Toronto, the story was part of a campaign to promote the arts sponsored by the city itself. Originally untitled, the story was given the title "The Zombie Who Liked the Arts" when it was included in a celebratory volume from Brown's publisher titled *Drawn & Quarterly: Twenty-Five Years of Contemporary Cartooning, Comics, and Graphic Novels* in 2015. Also included in that volume is the eight-page story "The Hymn of the Pearl," identified in its subtitle as "a comic-strip adaptation of an ancient narrative poem"

and part of a series of minicomics Brown is in the habit of creating for his friends, family, and Patreon supporters. Outside of Brown's self-published pamphlets, these short narratives remain unpublished and uncollected. One other prominent work for hire is Brown's cover design for the 2006 Penguin Classics Deluxe Edition of D. H. Lawrence's *Lady Chatterley's Lover*.

7. Although a real Saint Justin did exist, Brown has made it clear that the character is made up (see Torres, 79).

8. As Brown notes, this unusual approach means that "unlike most narrative print cartoonists, I *never* think about the page as a whole when I'm drawing. I think either about the individual panel or how it will work in a scene, but never about the page because I won't know which panels will go on which pages until I've finished everything and I'm assembling the work for publication" (qtd. in Evenson, 110; emphasis in the original).

CHAPTER 1: FROM OFF THE STREETS OF TORONTO COMES: *YUMMY FUR* THE MINICOMIC

1. See the introduction for an account of Brown's decision to shorten and abandon these two stories.

2. While "The Toilet Paper Revolt" was drawn in 1980, "Walrus Blubber Sandwich" was finished the next year. See the introduction for more on Brown's method of page composition and layout.

3. In a 1990 interview with Scott Grammel, Brown notes that as a child and teenager, "I was *very* uptight about my religious beliefs. That's the way we were brought up. Not only were we not allowed to say the Lord's name in vain, but we couldn't even say 'gosh.' I'm serious" (87; emphasis in the original). My account of Brown's upbringing and early career draws extensively on his generous answers in this interview.

4. To bridge the gap between issues, Brown published a collected edition of issues 1 through 6 of the minicomic in February 1985.

5. The seven issues of the *Yummy Fur* minicomic were reprinted in the first three issues of the identically titled but much longer run published first by Toronto's Vortex Comics and later by Drawn & Quarterly of Montreal. In order to refer to Brown's earliest material in its original context, in this chapter my references to these stories are to their first appearance in the minicomic. Most of Brown's early work (including almost everything I discuss in this book) has also been collected in the various editions of *Ed the Happy Clown* and in a collection of short strips titled *The Little Man*, all of which are significantly more accessible today than both runs of *Yummy Fur*.

6. See chapter 6 for a discussion of Brown's use of the pygmies, including his initial rationalization for their inclusion and his changing attitude to the concept of colonialism.

7. For Brown's full account of the creation of this strip, see the notes to the 2012 edition of *Ed the Happy Clown*.

8. Brown often goes by the name "Chet"; although the character is not meant to be self-representational, his name was inspired by Brown's fear of losing his drawing hand (see Torres, 79).

CHAPTER 2: SACRED PROFANITIES: *ED THE HAPPY CLOWN* AND THE GOSPEL ADAPTATIONS

1. In writing the piece, Luciano apparently became so fond of both the work he profiled and the word "dada" that he started his own "newave" anthology minicomic called *Dada Gumbo*. As described in chapter 1, it was Luciano who objected to Brown's inclusion of a drawing of dog shit in "Things to Avoid Stepping On," which in turn led Brown to create "The Man Who Couldn't Stop" as a further experiment in scatology. Luciano eventually published the strip unaltered in the seventh issue of *Dada Gumbo*, and Brown also contributed the story "Help Me Dear" to issue 8.

2. As Brown has pointed out, he had in fact been paid on one previous occasion, namely in 1973 when the local newspaper in Châteauguay paid the twelve-year-old Brown $7.50 for a five-panel gag strip, which it printed at the insistence of Brown's father. The strip is reprinted (along with an account of its publication) in the notes section of the 2006 edition of *The Little Man*, a collection of Brown's short work.

3. In the notes to the 2012 edition of *Ed the Happy Clown*, Brown recalls how Marks was further encouraged to sign *Yummy Fur* by the Toronto cartoonist Seth, who was drawing the series *Mister X* for Vortex. Although Brown and Seth were not yet friends (see chapter 3), Seth liked *Yummy Fur* and had been attempting to persuade Marks to publish it even before the review in the *Comics Journal*.

4. According to Brown, twelve thousand copies was "the highest order that a black-and-white Vortex comic-book had ever received" (*Ed* [2012], 215).

5. Accurately referencing the work making up the extended Ed the Happy Clown storyline is not a straightforward matter. As I describe briefly below (and discuss in more detail in chapter 6), in addition to its appearance in the Vortex run of *Yummy Fur* (some of which was itself originally published in the minicomics), the work has been collected in three very different book collections and a 2005 reserialization. In this chapter, I refer to the original appearance of the work in the Vortex editions of *Yummy Fur*.

6. When it was originally set to appear in *Yummy Fur*, the image showing Justin ejaculating onto his hand caused Marks to worry that the issue would be stopped at the US border, and he asked Brown to redraw it. Obstinate as ever, Brown recalls how "I decided that if I was going to be censored, I wanted my readers to know it was happening" (*Ed* [2012], 216). Instead of redrawing the panel, Brown partly covered the most offending parts with a written explanation and instructions to send him a

self-addressed envelope in order to receive a photocopy of the image. According to Brown, he received a few hundred such requests (see Evenson, 117). The original image appears uncensored in all the subsequent book collections of *Ed*.

7. As noted previously, Brown's Saint Justin is entirely his own creation and is not related to the historical figure (who lost his head rather than his hand). Although Brown did not model Chet on himself, he has acknowledged that this scene is inspired by childhood memories of his mother reading Bible stories to him and his brother (*Ed* [2012], 217).

8. Whereas the first installment of "Mark" was published in *Yummy Fur* issue 4 in April 1987 and the last in issue 14 in January 1989, the much longer but unfinished "Matthew" ran until the eleventh and final issue of *Underwater* in October 1997. Throughout this period, only a handful of issues did not contain an installment of the Gospel adaptations, while the thirty-second and last issue of *Yummy Fur* was entirely made up of a lengthy section of "Matthew."

9. Brown's interest in noncanonical Christian texts has also found expression in his short story "The Twin," which is based on a section from the ancient gnostic text *Pistis Sophia* and depicts Jesus's twin brother. Originally titled "Call of the Spirit" when it was published in the third issue of the Fantagraphics anthology comic *Prime Cuts* in 1987, Brown later changed the story's title and rearranged the panels to make up four rather than two pages for its inclusion in *The Little Man*.

10. As Brown impishly points out in the subsequent issue's letter column, "If I'd really wanted to overstate the case I could've drawn thirteen magi but it was easier to draw two" (*Yummy Fur* #16, 24).

11. In a 2011 interview, for example, Brown notes that although it "wouldn't be that difficult to finish Matthew at this point . . . my heart just isn't in it. I have no interest now in finishing it. There's other stuff I'd rather do" (qtd. in Rogers "A John's Gospel," n.p.). While he was in the middle of creating the narratives, Brown naturally felt differently and in issue 25 of *Yummy Fur* mentioned "a book collection of my MARK adaptation to be published by Vortex later next year" (*Yummy Fur* #25, 1). Since that book never materialized, Brown has more recently explained how "Bill [Marks] never paid me for the second edition of the Ed book, so I wasn't anxious to let him publish something else" (qtd. in Evenson, 123).

12. Having been nominated in several categories the previous year, in 1990 Brown won the Harvey Awards for "best cartoonist" and "best graphic album" for the 1989 edition of *Ed the Happy Clown*.

13. At the time, the closest Brown came to stating his opinion about the excised material was in the letter column for issue 28 of *Yummy Fur* (that is, a full ten issues after he dropped the storyline), in which he writes that "I've decided I don't feel like reprinting the Ed stuff in those issues and probably never will" (*Yummy Fur* #28, 28). More recently, Brown replied to the question of how he feels about the *Yummy Fur* version being lost to most readers with a single word: "Happy" (qtd. in Evenson, 109).

14. Although especially the early installments of *Yummy Fur*'s version of the narrative contain several references to Christian themes, Brown's assessment of the work also appears to be inspired by the new ending he first drew for the second book edition in 1992, in which Chet and Josie burn in hell for the sins of having killed each other (a feat accomplished by Josie after she is reanimated as a vampire). I discuss the different endings and Brown's motivations behind the changes in more detail in chapter 6.

15. Because the direct market system of distribution only tracks preorders by comic shops, final sales figures for *Yummy Fur* and other similarly distributed titles do not exist. The numbers I provide here are from Brown's discussion of preorders in Juno (135) and his notes to the 2012 edition of *Ed the Happy Clown* (*Ed* [2012], 238–39).

16. As with the decision to drop the title, Diamond's motives for resuming distribution of *Yummy Fur* remain unclear, but Brown has suggested that it was due to reporting on the issue by the *Comics Journal* (*Ed* [2012], 239). Brown notes about his income during these years that "I wasn't getting rich, but I was somehow able to pay my rent, keep myself fed, and avoid getting into debt. I had very low overhead and no expensive habits" (*Ed* [2012], 239).

CHAPTER 3: AUTOBIOGRAPHICAL DISCLOSURES: SHORT STORIES, *THE PLAYBOY*, AND *I NEVER LIKED YOU*

1. While "gerbil" initially seems like a randomly chosen word in this context, it was also Brown's nickname for his girlfriend Kris, who first encouraged him to self-publish his comics. In return, Kris called Brown "bunny," and for several years in the early run of *Yummy Fur* Brown occasionally drew himself as a rabbit in the comic's letter column.

2. Throughout the runs of both *Yummy Fur* and its successor *Underwater*, Brown was himself an enthusiastic supporter of his fellow alternative cartoonists, and often used his letter column to plug work by such creators as Julie Doucet, Joe Matt, Seth, Daniel Clowes, Colin Upton, Maurice Vellekoop, the Hernandez Brothers, Dave Sim, and Scott McCloud, among many others.

3. See Kunka for an authoritative overview of what he calls "proto-autobiographical comics" (22) from before the underground period.

4. Before he started work on the Pulitzer Prize–winning *Maus*, which was initially serialized in *Raw* from 1980 to 1991, Spiegelman published a short three-page story also titled "Maus" in the one-off underground comic *Funny Aminals* [sic] in 1972 and the four-page "Prisoner on the Hell Planet," about his mother's suicide, in the first issue of *Short Order Comix* in 1973. Although Pekar wrote the stories in *American Splendor*, they were drawn by a rotating roster of other artists, including, in one instance, Chester Brown. After Pekar had written—and Brown had illustrated—an untraditional foreword to the first book edition of *Ed the Happy Clown* in 1989, Brown illustrated a one-page story for issue 15 of *American Splendor*, in which the two artists

discuss Pekar's positive feelings about being paid three hundred dollars by Vortex's Bill Marks for that same foreword.

5. In my book *Serial Selves: Identity and Representation in Autobiographical Comics*, I discuss the genre's potential for personal expression and the working through of traumatic memories.

6. In issue 20, for example, Brown printed the following letter from "An Ex-YF Reader": "As for your feeble attempt at ripping off *American Splendor* in YF #19, all I can say is that it was a waste of $2. And a waste of my time. Pretty stupid idea." In the same issue, several other readers praised Brown's new direction with "Helder" in various ways, including that such stories "should be put into 'time capsules' for the 25th century" and that "if it's predictable then it isn't *Yummy Fur*" (*Yummy Fur* #20, 25, 26).

7. An early example of Brown's tendency to revise older material for republication, "Showing Helder" was extensively reformatted and redrawn when it was reprinted in the first edition of *The Little Man* in 1998. See chapter 6 for a discussion of Brown's revisions of his older work.

8. Brown makes this observation in the notes to the 2006 edition of *The Little Man* (169–70).

9. As Brown recalls, it was not only the subject matter itself of Matt's strip that inspired him to begin the story, but also what he saw as a fundamental flaw: "I recognized that the piece was courageous, but I also thought Joe was kidding himself if he actually believed he could so easily give up smut. That aspect of the . . . strip felt false to me and sparked the desire to write and draw an autobiographical strip about my experiences with *Playboy* and similar magazines" (*Playboy* [2013], 201). The Matt strip in question is dated "February 24th, 1988" and appears on page 6 of the various editions of *Peepshow: The Cartoon Diary of Joe Matt*.

10. For a discussion of the significant changes Brown made to the story between its various editions, see chapter 6.

11. As well as causing some discussion in the letter pages of *Yummy Fur*, the unusual technique was also depicted in Scott Russo and Jeff Wong's short parody-strip "Rancid Plotte," published in a special issue of the *Comics Journal* devoted to autobiographical comics in 1993.

12. One of the most intriguing responses to the work came from the publisher of *Playboy* magazine itself. As Brown has recalled, after the first book edition of *The Playboy* was published in 1992, he received a letter from Hugh Hefner, who "was surprised that anyone was still feeling guilty about that sort of stuff. He was sort of living in his own *Playboy* bubble world where he thought *Playboy* magazine and the sexual revolution in the 1960s had changed everything" (qtd. in McConnell, 203).

13. Although Matt's strips are presented as a "diary," their dates are unreliable and likely indicate when he began or finished work on them. As such, the "February 20th, 1991" strip shows Matt visiting Toronto, despite having already drawn an earlier strip about his permanent move to the city that is dated "October 25th, 1990."

14. In an obituary about Matt, who passed away in 2023, Jeet Heer offers the following assessment of how the three represented each other in their comics: "Together, they formed a strange embodied realization of the Freudian trinity: Joe was the id, pure untutored carnality; Brown, a libertarian, was the ego, the cagey pursuer of rational self-interest; Seth, the melancholy romantic, was the super-ego, the one who insisted on standards of moral conduct and artistic excellence" ("Farewell," n.p.).

15. While both Seth and Matt have often pointed out that their autobiographical work contains a large degree of fictionalization and sometimes even outright fabrication—with Seth's *It's a Good Life, If You Don't Weaken* being the prime example—Brown has been slightly more reticent in this respect, pointing instead to the essential subjectivity of all autobiography. In issue 28's letter column, for example, Brown responds to a reader praising the lack of "bias" in his stories by noting that "this is my version of what happened and not what *really* happened" (*Yummy Fur* #28, 28; emphasis in the original).

16. Although both Seth and Brown subsequently have produced work in other genres, Matt remained dedicated to autobiography until his death in 2023. A notoriously slow worker, Matt all but stopped publishing new comics after the fourteenth issue of *Peepshow* in 2006. After Matt's death, his friend and fellow cartoonist Sammy Harkham discovered that a fifteenth issue was nearly complete, with only four pages left to ink. In preparing the issue for publication, Harkham asked Brown to complete the final pages. In Brown's words, he "eagerly said yes. It should have been either me or Seth, and my style is closer to Joe's, so I was probably the obvious choice" ("Peep Show 15," n.p.). The issue was published by Fantagraphics in July 2024.

17. As it turns out, eating one's snot is far from unremarkable, and Brown has recalled how one of the most frequently asked questions he received from readers for some time after the story was published was "'do you really eat your snot?' The answer is yes" (*Little Man* [2006], 170). It probably did not help that the same issue's installment of "Matthew" features the apostle himself engaging in the same behavior.

18. Although the mother vaguely refers to her "mental difficulties" (*Yummy Fur* #30, 2) in the story, Brown has engaged with her diagnosis in his short story "My Mom Was a Schizophrenic," first published in issue 4 of *Underwater* and later collected in *The Little Man*. While her portrayal in Brown's autobiographical comics is often quite unflattering and seems indicative of a difficult maternal relationship, he has noted that her condition "didn't affect her ability to . . . be a good mom. I really couldn't have asked for a more perfect mother" (qtd. in Grammel, 69; ellipsis in the original). See chapter 4 for a discussion of "My Mom Was a Schizophrenic."

19. In Germany, however, a translated version of the narrative was published as *Fuck* by Jochen Enterprises in 1994, in an edition that also included the short story "The Little Man" (translated as "Der kleine Mann"). The same publisher also issued German translations of *Die Playboy-Stories* in 1992 and *Ed the Happy Clown* in 1993.

20. For a discussion of the revisions made to the second edition of *I Never Liked You*, see chapter 6.

21. The first Vortex edition of *Ed the Happy Clown* from 1989 was subtitled "A *Yummy Fur* Book."

22. Oliveros recalls that "because everything we published up until that time was comic books, the printing bill would never be that high. All of a sudden we're doing a book and the printing bill is five times higher than a normal comic book would be!" Deciding to take advantage of lower per unit prices for higher volume, Oliveros took a gamble and ordered "twelve thousand copies, because it's Chester, and it's a good book, and it's going to sell." Oliveros concludes the anecdote by noting that "it eventually did sell, but it took a long time" (qtd. in Rogers "Comic-Book Manufacturer," 65).

CHAPTER 4: TRANSITIONS: FROM *UNDERWATER* TO *LOUIS RIEL* AND THE GRAPHIC NOVEL

1. Although the story itself remains untitled, in *The Little Man* it is identified as "Knock Knock" in both the table of contents and the notes.

2. While issue 1 of *Underwater* is entirely made up of the first installment of the new storyline, Brown returned to "Matthew" for the second issue and continued the adaptation in the back pages for the duration of the series.

3. In issue 6's letter column, Brown writes that "I don't particularly want readers to waste large amounts of time trying to decipher the *Underwater* gibberish (and I hope it's not necessary to do so to enjoy the series) but those who do should find that it is possible to figure out 'Underwaterese'" (*Underwater* #6, 27). Elsewhere, Brown has made clear that the made-up language is "really just a code. Simple letter substitution" (qtd. in Verstappen, 173).

4. While Brown might not have originally intended the pacing of *Underwater* to be reflective of the infants' real-time development, the fact that it was serialized over three years means that this is not far from the case.

5. Sean Rogers, discussing the influence of Bresson on Brown's work in *Louis Riel*, offers the following: "'It is with something clean and precise,' Bresson writes, 'that you will force the attention of inattentive eyes and ears.' Brown uses precision and simplicity in much the same way: to direct attention, to cast things in an unaccustomed light, cleansed of what we thought we knew" ("Untitled Afterword," 329).

6. Toward the end of *Underwater*'s eleven-issue run, the always restless Brown once again began to change his visual approach. As such, most of the later issues have gray backgrounds and issues 10 and 11 even revert to the regular six-panel layout on white backgrounds familiar from Brown's earlier work.

7. Although Brown himself appears on the page, he is clearly speaking in an authorial voice and not as a character in an autobiographical story, for which reason I dispense with the distinction between Brown as author and Chester as character in my discussion of this story.

8. Throughout his serialized comic books, Brown's pagination is strikingly inconsistent, sometimes providing consecutive page numbers for an entire issue and sometimes restarting them with each new story installment. In issue four of *Underwater*, each of the three narratives have their own page numbers, and my reference here is to page 6 of this particular story and not the issue as a whole. The story is reprinted in *The Little Man*.

9. The two most notable of Brown's early polemical works are the short stories "Bob Crosby and His Electric T.V." (originally published in issue 3 of the minicomic version of *Yummy Fur* and reprinted in the first issue of the Vortex run) and "Catlick Creek" (published in issue 4 of the *Yummy Fur* minis and reprinted in the second Vortex issue). While the former is a critique of television as a medium, the latter concerns a real-life case where farmers in small-town Ontario were tricked into paying for the widening of a creek without any benefit to themselves. Speaking of "Catlick Creek," Brown has noted how he subsequently became uncomfortable with its overt didacticism: "I don't think it worked. It shouldn't have looked like I was just taking a story from real life and redoing it. It should've worked on its own merits or something" (qtd. in Grammel, 81). Perhaps for this reason, the story is not reprinted in *The Little Man*, despite seemingly falling under the criteria for inclusion established by Brown in that collection's preface.

10. "My Mom Was a Schizophrenic" was not originally intended for publication in *Underwater*. Rather, Brown had planned to self-publish the story as a minicomic and distribute it to phone booths and bus shelters across Toronto in the manner of Chick tracts (small religious pamphlets drawn and published by Jack Chick). Although he eventually included the story in *Underwater* in order to reach a larger readership, he still cycled around Toronto to leave a few hundred copies in public places. As Brown recalls, "one of those mini-comics ended up in the hands of someone who worked for the Mental Patients Association of Vancouver, and that organization asked if they could print the strip in their newsletter *In a Nutshell*. I agreed, of course" (*Little Man* [2006], 172).

11. Siggins's book is titled *Riel: A Life of Revolution* and was published in 1994. The full title of the book edition of Brown's work is *Louis Riel: A Comic-Strip Biography*."

12. Oliveros discusses the state of the comics market at the turn of the century in Rogers, "Comic-Book Manufacturer" 70–71. No other company was as influential in establishing the stand-alone graphic novel as a viable publishing category intended for bookstores as Drawn & Quarterly, and Oliveros even produced a pamphlet titled *Selling Graphic Novels in the Book Trade* with advice for store managers in 2003, the year of the first collected book edition of *Louis Riel*.

13. Simultaneously with his early work on *Louis Riel*, Brown also put together the first edition of *The Little Man*, a collection of his short narratives published in 1998. A second revised edition was published in 2006.

14. As Samantha Cutrara has shown, the result of Brown's highly selective focus is a distinct lack of representation of women in the narrative. Noting that "only 1.5% of the frames in *Louis Riel*, or 20 frames, features a woman who speaks or has a name," Cutrara also points out that a character as personally important as Riel's wife Marguerite Riel "is only seen twice in Brown's biography: pages 128 and 132" (124, 130).

15. As I discuss in chapters 5 and 6, Brown's politics changed substantially during the years he spent drawing *Louis Riel*, with the result that he came to see Macdonald in a more favorable light. For this reason, Brown even attempted a substantial rewrite of the story as he was nearing its conclusion, but when that proved too difficult he "just kept to the script that I had originally written and finished the book that way" (qtd. in Wivel, 161).

16. The orders for the later issues of the comic were down to around two thousand copies, a career-low for Brown except for the period when *Yummy Fur* was temporarily dropped by Diamond (see chapter 2). To aid him in completing the work under these difficult financial circumstances, Brown received a grant from the Canadian Council for the Arts in 2001, the first such grant to a comics artist. See chapter 6 for a discussion of Brown's revisions to the book edition of *Louis Riel*.

17. In Canada, a book is considered a bestseller when it has sold five thousand copies.

18. Throughout his career, Brown's work has been sporadically translated, with French and German editions being the most consistent.

CHAPTER 5: PROSTITUTION, POLITICS, AND THE BIBLE: *PAYING FOR IT* AND *MARY WEPT OVER THE FEET OF JESUS*

1. In 2001, Brown also worked on the 2002 revised edition of *I Never Liked You*, which swapped the black page backgrounds for white and added a short notes section that provided some biographical background information about the narrative. For a discussion of Brown's revisions to the book editions of *I Never Liked You*, see chapter 6. As Brown has explained, the idea of subtitling the 1992 edition of *Ed the Happy Clown* with "*The Definitive Ed Book*" came from Bill Marks, but Brown himself "wasn't absolutely sure that was the definitive version of the story. I still wasn't completely happy with the book's ending" (*Ed* #9, 23). (Providing page references for the reserialized edition of *Ed the Happy Clown* is potentially confusing since Brown numbered the entire nine-issue run consecutively, but without providing page numbers for his notes sections. When citing from these, I refer to the page of the individual issue, irrespective of the collected narrative's overall printed page numbers).

2. Brown has recalled how "it took a bit of effort to force myself back to *Riel*" (*Ed* #9, 23), and in light of his tendency to abandon work in progress in favor of working on something else, this moment seems significant to both the completion of *Louis Riel* and Brown's career as a whole.

3. Following the notes section in issue 9, Brown reprinted twelve penciled panels from the abandoned new version, taken from various points in the narrative. The most interesting change to be observed from this small sample is—as Brown himself points out in the notes—that he "chose the politically correct route and changed the rat-eating pygmies into mutant man-eating monkeys" (*Ed* #9, 24). To date, these twelve panels remain all that has been published of the new version of the narrative, and Brown seems to have made up his mind that "the 1992 definitive version *is* the definitive version of *Ed the Happy Clown*" (*Ed* #9, 24; emphasis in the original). For a discussion of the pygmies, including Brown's changing opinion of them, see chapter 6.

4. In addition to Brown's notes, the 2012 edition also includes several panels and sequences that were discarded when the narrative was originally serialized in *Yummy Fur*, as well as Brown's redrawn version of a short 1950s horror comic called "The Door," which had inspired a section of the Ed narrative.

5. The story of Dave Sim's fall from grace because of his misogyny is long and convoluted, and beyond the scope of this book. While Brown was friends with Sim for many years, in a note to the afterword in *Paying for It*, he mentions how "Dave Sim stopped regarding me as a friend in 2008 because I refused to sign an internet petition that he set up that reads, 'Dave Sim is not a misogynist.' I don't agree with his opinion that women are intellectually inferior to men, but my affection and respect for him remain unchanged" (*Paying for It* [2011], 276).

6. In the years since, Brown had remained close friends with Lee, who also wrote (with Joanne Sarazen) and directed the 2024 film adaptation of *Paying for It*, which was partly shot in the house the two once shared. Although film adaptations of *Ed the Happy Clown* and *Louis Riel* have been frequently discussed and optioned over the years, neither of these projects have come to fruition.

7. The title *Paying for It* was insisted upon by Brown's publisher Drawn & Quarterly, who objected to Brown's various other suggestions, including "23 Prostitutes," "I Pay for Sex," and "The Sex Life of John Brown." In a note, Brown admits to not liking the book's title, because, as he says, "there's an implied double-meaning. It suggests that not only am I paying for sex but I am also paying for being a john in some non-monetary way. Many would think that there's an emotional cost—that johns are sad and lonely" (*Paying for It* [2011], 259). Two of Brown's preferred titles survive in the French and German editions, respectively titled *Vingt-trois prostituées* and *Ich bezahle für Sex*. In addition to these, translations have been published in Italian, Spanish, Czech, and Serbian.

8. The legal status of prostitution in Canada eventually appears as a main topic in the work, but in the foreword Brown explains "the legal situation . . . during the years covered by this memoir: 'Outcall' prostitution was legal—that is, sex-workers were allowed to go to a john's home or hotel room. 'Incall' prostitution was illegal—sex-workers were not allowed to work out of a specific location" (*Paying for It* [2011], ix). In the additional notes written for the 2024 "film edition" of the book, Brown

explains how the situation has since changed: "In 2014 the Canadian government brought 'the Swedish model' of sex-work criminalization to the country I live in. It's now illegal to pay someone for sex. But it *is* legal for someone to *accept* payment for sex" (296; emphases in the original). Brown continues to observe the implication that "I'm *probably* committing a crime by paying 'Denise' for sex, and she's definitely *not* committing a crime by accepting that payment. I'm not totally sure that my friendship with 'Denise' really would fall under the law's purview. When the legislators crafted the 2014 law, I doubt that they had in mind a 21-year monogamous relationship in which the person being paid for sex states that she doesn't consider herself a sex-worker" (296; emphases in the original).

9. Although *Paying for It*'s unusual mix of traditional first-person comics narrative and extensive authorial notes can sometimes make the distinction difficult to uphold, I continue to refer to the character as Chester and the author as Brown in my discussion of the book.

10. The only variation from the grid is when Brown occasionally ends a chapter with a single panel centered on the page, as if to punctuate the previous sequence slightly differently.

11. So committed is Brown to his emotionally neutral style that instead of giving himself a different facial expression after a particularly contentious argument with his friend Seth, he resorts to drawing a cartoony lightning storm in a thought bubble above his head in order to indicate anger.

12. In the original 2011 hardback edition, the paratextual material includes an introduction by Robert Crumb, a foreword and an afterword by Brown himself, twenty-three appendices (the last of which contains Seth's response to the book), a lengthy notes section, and a bibliography. For the 2013 paperback edition, Brown removed the Crumb introduction but added another ten pages of notes, including a separate bibliography. In addition to the hardback and paperback editions of *Paying for It*, a new "film edition" was published in 2024, with a new introduction by Lee (who cowrote and directed the film). True to Brown's habit of adding supplementary notes and other material to each new edition of his work, this version includes several new pages in which he comments on his continuing relationship with "Denise," describes a few other sexual encounters, discusses the legal status of prostitution in Canada, and considers the changes to the story made for the film. In addition, the expanded notes section also features such material as scenes deleted from the original comic, production stills from the film, and Brown's drawings of several cast members. Most noteworthy of the new additions are three pages from Brown's first attempt to draw the book, in a style that differs significantly from its eventual published form and predates Brown's appreciation for Fletcher Hanks. For a discussion of Brown's career-long use of paratextual material such as notes and letter columns to engage with readers and shape the reception of his work, see chapter 6.

13. Bethell, a longtime senior editor of the *American Spectator* and a fellow of the conservative think tank the Hoover Institution, promoted many controversial theories throughout his career, including the fallacy of Darwinian evolution, the idea that HIV does not cause AIDS, the denial of man-made global warming, and that Edward de Vere was the real author of the works credited to William Shakespeare.

14. Despite the low numbers, Brown is quick to point out that "I got more votes than any other Libertarian Party candidate across Canada" (qtd. in Gilson, 233). Elsewhere, Brown has acknowledged that his main motivation for running is to draw attention to Libertarian causes: "I know there's no way I'm going to win. If I get 1 percent of the vote, I'll be happy" (qtd. in Murray, 224).

15. As Brown has made clear in both the notes to the 2024 "film edition" of the book and in blog posts available to his Patreon supporters, he has been paying "Denise" for sex for over twenty years, and the two are still monogamous with each other.

16. As Khan points out, while Brown's relationship with Denise in some ways resembles the relationship between a sugar daddy and a sugar baby, "their relational history as client to sex worker, Brown's precarious work as a cartoonist, his tight budget and humble mode of transportation (cycling), their relative closeness in age (less than 10 years), along with the fact that 'Denise' has, in Brown's words, a 'regular nine-to-five job,' does not fit the 'sugar' paradigm of age, economic and status asymmetries" (60).

17. See chapter 6 for a discussion of the revised edition of *The Playboy*.

18. As Brown has said, the large heads are partly a result of the book's small format: "I wanted the book to be small, and originally it was going to be even smaller than it is now. So I was thinking, to keep the characters recognizable (especially since there are so many different characters), that I should draw the heads larger than I had in the last two books" (qtd. in Bagge, n.p.).

19. Although it is drawn in a style similar to the rest of the book, Brown's version of "Job" is formatted according to a different and less regular grid. As such, it gives the impression that it was originally conceived for a different project, likely one of the self-published minicomics Brown is in the habit of creating for his family, friends, and Patreon supporters.

20. Hatfield, commenting on the additional material, points out that "these voluminous notes seem to want to *reason* with the reader, whereas the comics want to provoke and challenge" ("Review," n.p.; emphasis in the original).

CHAPTER 6: RETCONNING CHESTER BROWN: REVISIONS, NOTES, AND AUTHORIAL VOICE

1. According to Ng Suat Tong, writing in the *Comics Journal*, this discrepancy is in fact "an age-old and complicated dispute which involves varying manuscripts and the possible misidentification of the village of Khersa" (32). By neglecting to mention that history in favor of suggesting to the reader that "if you whip out your Bible maps you'll

see that Gerasa is nowhere near a sea of any kind" (*Yummy Fur* #8, 26), Brown (perhaps slightly naively) presents himself as responsible for discovering the discrepancy.

2. This tendency has also found expression in his notes to *Chester Brown: Conversations*, a book of collected interviews. Commenting on interviews conducted many years earlier, Brown offers such assessments that "I now disagree with this statement" and "I lied in this answer" (qtd. in Grace and Hoffman *Conversations*, 51n, 87n).

3. In fact, this practice is so unusual that it was only after seeing the notes to the Gospel adaptations in *Yummy Fur* that Alan Moore was inspired to include endnotes in *From Hell*, arguably the most famous such instance (see Grace and Hoffman "Introduction," xiv).

4. In this context, it is worth noting that in the new but ultimately abandoned version of the narrative Brown worked on in 2004 (see chapter 5), he replaced the pygmies with monkeys.

5. As Brown recalls, he initially intended to use the head of Ed Broadbent, the leader of the left-wing New Democratic Party in Canada, because of Broadbent's "aggressive, rude, and generally obnoxious" (*Ed* [2012], 223) performance in a 1979 federal election debate.

6. For a very thorough review of the publication history and extensive changes made between the many different editions of the Ed the Happy Clown narrative, see Evenson.

7. Considering his extensive revisions to nearly all his early work, which include relettering *The Playboy* for the 2013 book edition, the single most confounding note in Brown's oeuvre may be when he points out two small spelling mistakes in the 2012 version of *Ed the Happy Clown* before adding that "I'm not bothering to fix them" (*Ed* [2012], 237).

8. Occasionally, as Brown points out in the notes to the 2012 edition of *Ed the Happy Clown*, this method of composition presents "the danger that panels won't 'work' together" (*Ed* [2012], 221). In order to illustrate this issue, Brown includes two panels as he originally intended to present them, where "the juxtaposition is awkward—it looks to me like an odd elongated figure with Josie's head and Ed's body" (*Ed* [2012], 221).

9. Although Brown significantly changed the ending for the 1992 book version, only a short section was redrawn to fit the new conclusion.

10. In a reflection of the developing publication models for comics over the last few decades, Brown has repeatedly changed his mind about how to describe the collected versions of his earlier work. *The Playboy*, for example, adjusted its subtitle from "a comic book" to "a comic-strip memoir" between its two book editions, while *Ed the Happy Clown* moved from being "a *Yummy Fur* book" to "a comic book" before graduating to "graphic-novel" between its three editions in 1989, 1992, and 2012.

11. Regarding the tendency of his books to get physically smaller with each edition, Brown has said in an interview conducted for the publication of *Mary Wept Over the*

Feet of Jesus that "I can't say that there was a good reason for wanting the book to be small. I just like small books" (qtd. in Bagge, n.p.). Similarly, Brown has commented about the significant decrease in the size of the artwork itself for the 2012 edition of *Ed the Happy Clown*: "The smaller the better, as long as the words are still legible" (qtd. in Evenson, 111). Curiously, the book itself is roughly the same size as the 1989 and 1992 editions, but the drastically enlarged margins mean that the drawings are surrounded by large amounts of white space, giving a more austere impression in line with Brown's more recent work. Brown used a similar approach for the thoroughly revised 2013 edition of *The Playboy*.

12. In the notes to the 2013 edition, Brown further reframes the scene by noting that "through Playmates like Deborah Borkman, Azizi Johari, and Rosanne Katon, *Playboy* helped this white kid, who grew up in an almost all-white suburb, to see the sexual appeal of non-white women" (*Playboy* [2013], 213). For a one-page strip titled "Racism" that appeared before the first installment of "Disgust" in the twenty-first issue of *Yummy Fur*, Brown had originally contextualized the scene by providing an account of the racism exhibited by people close to him during his childhood.

13. Regarding the changes made to the new edition, Brown notes that "besides rearranging the word-balloons and rewriting many of them, I've also removed certain panels that appeared in previous editions of *The Playboy*. But don't worry, you're not missing any of that artwork; I'm printing all of the deleted panels in this notes section" (*Playboy* 1994, 205). By focusing on the missing panels, this inclusion nevertheless obscures the fact of Brown's silent redrawing of several key panels.

14. While Brown evidently expended a large amount of creative time and energy on the 2013 edition of *The Playboy*, it is noteworthy that it is missing from a list of "some of my graphic novels" on his Patreon page, which otherwise includes all his collected long-form narratives.

15. In *Yummy Fur*, the narrative begins with a nine-year-old Chester addressing the reader to explain his habit of "taking real words and changing them into nonsense words," which functions to set up the scene in which he greets Connie with "I *shit* it was you" (*Yummy Fur* #26, 2, 3). Although Brown remembers Seth telling him that "it works better if the audience knows why I'm saying that" (qtd. in Sim "Chester Brown," 191), he ignored that advice and removed the sequence when assembling the narrative for the book editions.

16. For Brown's description of the visual revisions to the collected version of *Louis Riel*, see the notes to the "tenth anniversary edition" from 2013, which also includes several examples.

17. As described in chapter 5, Brown has continued to expand the notes section in *Paying for It* with each new edition, most recently for the 2024 "film edition."

18. In addition to blog posts, Brown also regularly sends his patrons hard copy minicomics in the mail, which arrive in tiny envelopes addressed in Brown's distinctive handwriting. As an example of Carney's "private communiqué," these minicomics

are unpublished elsewhere and have in a sense allowed Brown to come full circle and return to his roots in the early 1980s minicomic scene.

19. In July 2024, Brown had 211 paying patrons and received a total of US $616 per month. While this places him somewhere in the middle of comics creators on Patreon, the numbers are substantially lower than those of such top-ten figures as Jeph Jacques (12,344 patrons) and Kate Beaton (2,768 patrons), who Graphtreon (an unaffiliated site offering charts and other analysis) estimates to receive monthly pledges respectively worth US $22,000–$86,000 and US $5,000–$18,000.

20. Most recently (and more publicly), Brown has casually referred to "the covid hoax" and said that he "knew covid wasn't real" when describing his nonsexual encounter with a sex worker in the notes to the 2024 "film edition" of *Paying for It* (296).

CONCLUSION: AGAINST THE GRAIN

1. Despite the controversial nature of much of his work and public persona, Brown's status and overall respectability was further underlined when he was one of the Canadian comics artists featured on a series of four Canada Post stamps released in May 2024 (the others being Seth, Michel Rabagliati, and the creative team of cousins Jillian and Mariko Tamaki). The stamp, for which Brown created new artwork, features a drawing of Louis Riel reading Brown's biography of him.

BIBLIOGRAPHY

Bagge, Peter. “An Interview with Chester Brown.” *Comics Journal*, June 6, 2016, www.tcj.com/an-interview-with-chester-brown.

Beaty, Bart. “Selective Mutual Reinforcement in the Comics of Chester Brown, Joe Matt, and Seth.” *Graphic Subjects: Critical Essays on Autobiography and Graphic Novels*, edited by Michael A. Chaney, U of Wisconsin P, 2011, pp. 247–59.

Boyd, Robert. “Seasonal Disorder: Spring with Drawn & Quarterly.” *Comics Journal*, no. 198, 1997, pp. 41–44.

Brogan, Jacob. “‘The Bible Is Inexhaustible’: Chester Brown on His Cartoon Exploration of Jesus and Prostitution.” *Slate*, April 8, 2016, www.slate.com/culture/2016/04/interview-with-cartoonist-chester-brown-about-jesus-mary-and-sex-work.html.

Brown, Chester. *Ed the Happy Clown* #1. Drawn & Quarterly, 2005.

Brown, Chester. *Ed the Happy Clown* #2. Drawn & Quarterly, 2005.

Brown, Chester. *Ed the Happy Clown* #3. Drawn & Quarterly, 2005.

Brown, Chester. *Ed the Happy Clown* #4. Drawn & Quarterly, 2005.

Brown, Chester. *Ed the Happy Clown* #5. Drawn & Quarterly, 2006.

Brown, Chester. *Ed the Happy Clown* #6. Drawn & Quarterly, 2006.

Brown, Chester. *Ed the Happy Clown* #7. Drawn & Quarterly, 2006.

Brown, Chester. *Ed the Happy Clown* #8. Drawn & Quarterly, 2006.

Brown, Chester. *Ed the Happy Clown* #9. Drawn & Quarterly, 2006.

Brown, Chester. *Ed the Happy Clown: A Comic Book* [“The Definitive Ed Book”]. Vortex Comics, 1992.

Brown, Chester. *Ed the Happy Clown: A Graphic-Novel*. Drawn & Quarterly, 2012.

Brown, Chester. *Ed the Happy Clown: A Yummy Fur Book*. Vortex Comics, 1989.

Brown, Chester. *I Never Liked You: A Comic Book*. Drawn & Quarterly, 1994.

Brown, Chester. *I Never Liked You: A Comic-Strip Narrative*. Drawn & Quarterly, 2002.

Brown, Chester. *The Little Man: Short Strips, 1980–1995*. Drawn & Quarterly, 1998.

Brown, Chester. *The Little Man: Short Strips, 1980–1995*. Drawn & Quarterly, 2006.

Brown, Chester. *Louis Riel* #1. Drawn & Quarterly, 1999.

Brown, Chester. *Louis Riel* #2. Drawn & Quarterly, 1999.

Brown, Chester. *Louis Riel* #3. Drawn & Quarterly, 1999.

Brown, Chester. *Louis Riel* #4. Drawn & Quarterly, 2000.

Brown, Chester. *Louis Riel* #5. Drawn & Quarterly, 2000.

Brown, Chester. *Louis Riel* #6. Drawn & Quarterly, 2001.

Brown, Chester. *Louis Riel* #7. Drawn & Quarterly, 2002.

Brown, Chester. *Louis Riel* #8. Drawn & Quarterly, 2002.

Brown, Chester. *Louis Riel* #9. Drawn & Quarterly, 2003.

Brown, Chester. *Louis Riel* #10. Drawn & Quarterly, 2003.

Brown, Chester. *Louis Riel: A Comic-Strip Biography*. Drawn & Quarterly, 2003.

Brown, Chester. *Louis Riel: A Comic-Strip Biography* ["Tenth Anniversary Edition"]. Drawn & Quarterly, 2013.

Brown, Chester. *Mary Wept Over the Feet of Jesus*. Drawn & Quarterly, 2016.

Brown, Chester. "My Response to Salgood." *Patreon*, May 10, 2020, www.patreon.com/posts/my-response-to-36967232.

Brown, Chester. *Paying for It: A Comic-Strip Memoir about Being a John*. Drawn & Quarterly, 2011.

Brown, Chester. *Paying for It: A Comic-Strip Memoir about Being a John*. Drawn & Quarterly, 2013.

Brown, Chester. *Paying for It: A Comic-Strip Memoir about Being a John* ["Film Edition"]. Drawn & Quarterly, 2024.

Brown, Chester. "Peep Show 15." *Patreon*, May 16, 2024, https://www.patreon.com/posts/peep-show-15-104359391.

Brown, Chester. *The Playboy: A Comic Book*. Drawn & Quarterly, 1992.

Brown, Chester. *The Playboy: A Comic-Strip Memoir*. Drawn & Quarterly, 2013.

Brown, Chester. "Pwyll and the Other World, panel 14:3." *Patreon*, September 20, 2019, www.patreon.com/posts/pwyll-and-other-30091661.

Brown, Chester. *Underwater* #1. Drawn & Quarterly, 1994.

Brown, Chester. *Underwater* #2. Drawn & Quarterly, 1994.

Brown, Chester. *Underwater* #3. Drawn & Quarterly, 1995.

Brown, Chester. *Underwater* #4. Drawn & Quarterly, 1995.

Brown, Chester. *Underwater* #5. Drawn & Quarterly, 1996.

Brown, Chester. *Underwater* #6. Drawn & Quarterly, 1996.

Brown, Chester. *Underwater* #7. Drawn & Quarterly, 1996.

Brown, Chester. *Underwater* #8. Drawn & Quarterly, 1996.

Brown, Chester. *Underwater* #9. Drawn & Quarterly, 1997.

Brown, Chester. *Underwater* #10. Drawn & Quarterly, 1997.

Brown, Chester. *Underwater* #11. Drawn & Quarterly, 1997.

Brown, Chester. *Yummy Fur* #1 [minicomic]. Tortured Canoe, 1983.

Brown, Chester. *Yummy Fur* #2 [minicomic]. Tortured Canoe, 1983.

Brown, Chester. *Yummy Fur* #3 [minicomic]. Tortured Canoe, 1983.

Brown, Chester. *Yummy Fur* #4 [minicomic]. Tortured Canoe, 1983.

Brown, Chester. *Yummy Fur* #5 [minicomic]. Tortured Canoe, 1984.

Brown, Chester. *Yummy Fur* #6 [minicomic]. Tortured Canoe, 1984.

Brown, Chester. *Yummy Fur* #7 [minicomic]. Tortured Canoe, 1985.

Brown, Chester. *Yummy Fur* #1. Vortex Comics, 1986.
Brown, Chester. *Yummy Fur* #2. Vortex Comics, 1987.
Brown, Chester. *Yummy Fur* #3. Vortex Comics, 1987.
Brown, Chester. *Yummy Fur* #4. Vortex Comics, 1987.
Brown, Chester. *Yummy Fur* #5. Vortex Comics, 1987.
Brown, Chester. *Yummy Fur* #6. Vortex Comics, 1987.
Brown, Chester. *Yummy Fur* #7. Vortex Comics, 1987.
Brown, Chester. *Yummy Fur* #8. Vortex Comics, 1987.
Brown, Chester. *Yummy Fur* #9. Vortex Comics, 1988.
Brown, Chester. *Yummy Fur* #10. Vortex Comics, 1988.
Brown, Chester. *Yummy Fur* #11. Vortex Comics, 1988.
Brown, Chester. *Yummy Fur* #12. Vortex Comics, 1988.
Brown, Chester. *Yummy Fur* #13. Vortex Comics, 1988.
Brown, Chester. *Yummy Fur* #14. Vortex Comics, 1989.
Brown, Chester. *Yummy Fur* #15. Vortex Comics, 1989.
Brown, Chester. *Yummy Fur* #16. Vortex Comics, 1989.
Brown, Chester. *Yummy Fur* #17. Vortex Comics, 1989.
Brown, Chester. *Yummy Fur* #18. Vortex Comics, 1989.
Brown, Chester. *Yummy Fur* #19. Vortex Comics, 1990.
Brown, Chester. *Yummy Fur* #20. Vortex Comics, 1990.
Brown, Chester. *Yummy Fur* #21. Vortex Comics, 1990.
Brown, Chester. *Yummy Fur* #22. Vortex Comics, 1990.
Brown, Chester. *Yummy Fur* #23. Vortex Comics, 1990.
Brown, Chester. *Yummy Fur* #24. Vortex Comics, 1991.
Brown, Chester. *Yummy Fur* #25. Drawn & Quarterly, 1991.
Brown, Chester. *Yummy Fur* #26. Drawn & Quarterly, 1991.
Brown, Chester. *Yummy Fur* #27. Drawn & Quarterly, 1992.
Brown, Chester. *Yummy Fur* #28. Drawn & Quarterly, 1992.
Brown, Chester. *Yummy Fur* #29. Drawn & Quarterly, 1992.
Brown, Chester. *Yummy Fur* #30. Drawn & Quarterly, 1993.
Brown, Chester. *Yummy Fur* #31. Drawn & Quarterly, 1993.
Brown, Chester. *Yummy Fur* #32. Drawn & Quarterly, 1994.
Carney, Sean. "The Ear of the Eye, or, Do Drawings Make Sounds?" *English Language Notes*, vol. 46, no. 2, 2008, pp. 193–209.
Coody, Elizabeth Rae. "The Ending of Mark as a Page-turn Reveal." *Comics and Sacred Texts: Reimagining Religion and Graphic Narratives*, edited by Assaf Gamzou and Ken Koltun-Fromm, UP of Mississippi, 2018, pp. 98–112.
Costello, Brannon, and Brian Cremins. "'Avenues of Free Thought and Fellow Feeling': U.S. Comic Books in the 1980s." *The Other 1980s: Reframing Comics' Crucial Decade*, edited by Brannon Costello and Brian Cremins, Louisiana State UP, 2021, pp. 1–19.

Cutrara, Samantha. "Drawn out of History: The Representation of Women in Chester Brown's *Louis Riel: A Comic-Strip Biography*." *Graphic History: Essays on Graphic Novels and/as History*, edited by Richard Iadonisi, Cambridge Scholars Publishing, 2012, pp. 121–43.

Daly, Mark. "Seth, Brown, Matt." *Comics Journal*, no. 162, 1993, pp. 51–56.

Editors, the. "A *Clyde Fans* Roundtable." *Comics Journal*, June 6, 2019, https://www.tcj.com/a-clyde-fans-roundtable.

Epp, Darrell. "Two-Handed Man Interviews Cartoonist Chester Brown." *Chester Brown: Conversations*, edited by Dominick Grace and Eric Hoffman, UP of Mississippi, 2013, pp. 118–47.

Evenson, Brian. *Ed vs. Yummy Fur: Or, What Happens When a Serial Comic Becomes a Graphic Novel*. Uncivilized Books, 2014.

Gilson, Dave. "The Pickup Artist: An Interview with Chester Brown." *Chester Brown: Conversations*, edited by Dominick Grace and Eric Hoffman, UP of Mississippi, 2013, pp. 228–34.

Grace, Dominick, and Eric Hoffman, editors. *Chester Brown: Conversations*. UP of Mississippi, 2013.

Grace, Dominick, and Eric Hoffman, editors. "Introduction." *Chester Brown: Conversations*, edited by Dominick Grace and Eric Hoffman, UP of Mississippi, 2013, pp. vii–xxxi.

Grace, Dominick, and Eric Hoffman, editors. "Introduction: Comics in Canada." *The Canadian Alternative: Cartoonists, Comics, and Graphic Novels from the North*, edited by Dominick Grace and Eric Hoffman, UP of Mississippi, 2017, pp. ix–xix.

Grammel, Scott. "Chester Brown: From the Sacred to the Scatological." *Comics Journal*, no. 135, 1990, pp. 66–90.

Groth, Gary. "Seth." *Comics Journal*, no. 193, 1997, pp. 58–93.

Hair, Lee. "Friends, Not ATMs: Parasocial Relational Work and the Construction of Intimacy by Artists on Patreon." *Sociological Spectrum*, vol. 41, no. 2, 2021, pp. 196–212.

Hall, James C. "'Say "Shit" Chester': Language, Alienation, and the Aesthetic in Chester Brown's *I Never Liked You: A Comic-Strip Narrative*." *Canadian Graphic: Picturing Life Narratives*, edited by Candida Rifkind and Linda Warley, Wilfrid Laurier UP, 2016, pp. 99–126.

Hatfield, Charles. *Alternative Comics: An Emerging Literature*. UP of Mississippi, 2005.

Hatfield, Charles. "The Autobiographical Stories in *Yummy Fur*." *Comics Journal*, no. 210, 1999, p. 67.

Hatfield, Charles. "Review: *Mary Wept Over the Feet of Jesus*." *Comics Journal*, April 13, 2016, www.tcj.com/reviews/mary-wept-over-the-feet-of-jesus.

Heer, Jeet. "Farewell to a Poor Bastard." *The Nation*, September 21, 2023, https://www.thenation.com/article/culture/joe-matt-cartoonist-obituary.

Heer, Jeet. "A Makeshift Tradition: Canada's Cartooning Heritage." *This is Serious: Canadian Indie Comics*, edited by Alana Traficante and Joe Ollmann, Conundrum Press, 2019, pp. 10–13.

Joe Shuster Awards. "Brown, Chester (1960–)." 2011, www.joeshusterawards.com/hof/brown-chester-1960.

Juno, Andrea. *Dangerous Drawings: Interviews with Comix & Graphix Artists*. Juno Books, 1997.

Khan, Ummni. "Chester Brown and the Queerness of Johns." *Critical Analysis of Law*, vol. 6, no. 1, 2019, pp. 39–62.

Köhler, Nicholas. "Chester Brown on Prostitution, Romantic Love, and Being a John." *Chester Brown: Conversations*, edited by Dominick Grace and Eric Hoffman, UP of Mississippi, 2013, pp. 210–14.

Køhlert, Frederik Byrn. *Serial Selves: Identity and Representation in Autobiographical Comics*. Rutgers UP, 2019.

Kreider, Tim. "Wages of Love: Chester Brown's True Romance Comix." *Comics Journal*, vol. 302, 2013, pp. 505–14.

Kunka, Andrew J. *Autobiographical Comics*. Bloomsbury, 2018.

Lanzendörfer, Tim. "Biographiction: Narratological Aspects of Chester Brown's *Louis Riel*." *Zeitschrift fur Anglistik und Amerikanistik*, vol. 59, no. 1, 2011, pp. 27–40.

Lehoczky, Etelka. "God And Sex Workers—Plus Cartoons—In 'Mary Wept.'" *NPR*, April 16, 2016, www.npr.org/2016/04/16/471621997/god-and-sex-workers-plus-cartoons-in-mary-wept.

Lesk, Andrew. "Redrawing Nationalism: Chester Brown's *Louis Riel: A Comic-Strip Biography*." *Journal of Graphic Novels & Comics*, vol. 1, no. 1, 2010, pp. 63–81.

Lethem, Jonathan. "A Furtive Exchange." *Drawn & Quarterly: Twenty-Five Years of Contemporary Cartooning, Comics, and Graphic Novels*, edited by Tom Devlin, Drawn & Quarterly, 2015, pp. 131–33.

Levin, Bob. "Good Ol' Chester Brown." *Comics Journal*, no. 162, 1993, pp. 45–49.

Luciano, Dale. "Newave Comics Survey." *Comics Journal*, no. 96, 1985, pp. 51–78.

Matt, Joe. *Peepshow: The Cartoon Diary of Joe Matt*. Drawn & Quarterly, 2003.

McConnell, Robin. "Chester Brown." *Chester Brown: Conversations*, edited by Dominick Grace and Eric Hoffman, UP of Mississippi, 2013, pp. 194–209.

McGillis, Ian. "Laying It Bare: An Interview with Chester Brown." *Chester Brown: Conversations*, edited by Dominick Grace and Eric Hoffman, UP of Mississippi, 2013, pp. 215–18.

Miller, Nicholas E. "'Now That It's Just Us Girls': Transmedial Feminisms from *Archie* to *Riverdale*." *Feminist Media Histories*, vol. 4, no. 3, 2018, pp. 205–26.

Monaco, Steve. "M-mm Good." *Comics Journal*, no. 107, 1986, pp. 53–55.

Moreton, Andrew, et al. "Chester Brown." *Chester Brown: Conversations*, edited by Dominick Grace and Eric Hoffman, UP of Mississippi, 2013, pp. 3–23.

Murray, Noel. "Interview: Chester Brown." *Chester Brown: Conversations*, edited by Dominick Grace and Eric Hoffman, UP of Mississippi, 2013, pp. 219–27.

Postema, Barbara. *Narrative Structure in Comics: Making Sense of Fragments*. RIT Press, 2013.

Rifkind, Candida. "Louis Riel: An Appreciation." *Drawn & Quarterly: Twenty-Five Years of Contemporary Cartooning, Comics, and Graphic Novels*, edited by Tom Devlin, Drawn & Quarterly, 2015, pp. 136–37.

Rogers, Sean. "The Comic-Book Manufacturer." *Drawn & Quarterly: Twenty-Five Years of Contemporary Cartooning, Comics, and Graphic Novels*, edited by Tom Devlin, Drawn & Quarterly, 2015, pp. 61–73.

Rogers, Sean. "A History of Drawn & Quarterly." *Drawn & Quarterly: Twenty-Five Years of Contemporary Cartooning, Comics, and Graphic Novels*, edited by Tom Devlin, Drawn & Quarterly, 2015, pp. 13–57.

Rogers, Sean. "A John's Gospel: The Chester Brown Interview." *Comics Journal*, May 9, 2011, www.tcj.com/a-johns-gospel-the-chester-brown-interview.

Rogers, Sean. "Untitled Afterword." *Louis Riel: Tenth Anniversary Edition*, Drawn & Quarterly, 2013, pp. 325–31.

Russo, Scott, and Jeff Wong. "Rancid Plotte." *Comics Journal*, no. 162, 1993, pp. 79–82.

Sim, Dave. *Cerebus* #186. Aardvark-Vanaheim, 1994.

Sim, Dave. "Chester Brown." *Chester Brown: Conversations*, edited by Dominick Grace and Eric Hoffman, UP of Mississippi, 2013, pp. 182–93.

Smyth, Fiona. "From Sad Clowns to Psychedooolia." *Canadian Literature*, no. 249, 2022, pp. 146–55.

Solomos, Steve. "Shades of Brown." *Chester Brown: Conversations*, edited by Dominick Grace and Eric Hoffman, UP of Mississippi, 2013, pp. 86–117.

Tong, Ng Suat. "Chester Brown's Gospels: *Mark* and *Matthew*." *Comics Journal*, no. 261, 2004, pp. 31–37.

Torres, Jay. "Chester Brown." *Chester Brown: Conversations*, edited by Dominick Grace and Eric Hoffman, UP of Mississippi, 2013, pp. 73–85.

Tousley, Nancy. "Chester Brown: Louis Riel's Comic-Strip Biographer." *Chester Brown: Conversations*, edited by Dominick Grace and Eric Hoffman, UP of Mississippi, 2013, pp. 176–81.

Verstappen, Nicolas. "Chester Brown." *Chester Brown: Conversations*, edited by Dominick Grace and Eric Hoffman, UP of Mississippi, 2013, pp. 168–75.

Williams, Dylan. "An Interview with Seth." *Seth: Conversations*, edited by Eric Hoffman and Dominick Grace, UP of Mississippi, 2015, pp. 7–67.

Williams, Paul. *Dreaming the Graphic Novel: The Novelization of Comics*. Rutgers UP, 2020.

Wivel, Matthias. "On the Real: An Interview with Chester Brown." *Chester Brown: Conversations*, edited by Dominick Grace and Eric Hoffman, UP of Mississippi, 2013, pp. 156–67.

Young, Frank. "Peeping Joe." *Comics Journal*, no. 149, 1992, pp. 37–40.

INDEX

Page numbers in *italic* refer to images.

ABOUT THE AUTHOR

Credit: Photo courtesy of the author

Frederik Byrn Køhlert is lecturer in English and Film at Edinburgh Napier University. He is the author of *Serial Selves: Identity and Representation in Autobiographical Comics*, as well as several articles and book chapters on comics and related visual media. In addition, he is the author and editor of two books on the literary and cultural history of Chicago.

www.ingramcontent.com/pod-product-compliance
Lightning Source LLC
LaVergne TN
LVHW020823280325
806768LV00002B/7

* 9 7 8 1 4 9 6 8 5 8 3 4 4 *